The Final Word

The Final Word

A True Account of Murder and Redemption

by
JENNY TAYLOR

RESOURCE *Publications* · Eugene, Oregon

THE FINAL WORD
A True Account of Murder and Redemption

Edited by Adria Vaughan.

Copyright © 2025 Jenny Taylor. All rights reserved. Except for brief quotations in critical publications or reviews, no part of this book may be reproduced in any manner without prior written permission from the publisher. Write: Permissions, Wipf and Stock Publishers, 199 W. 8th Ave., Suite 3, Eugene, OR 97401.

Resource Publications
An Imprint of Wipf and Stock Publishers
199 W. 8th Ave., Suite 3
Eugene, OR 97401

www.wipfandstock.com

PAPERBACK ISBN: 979-8-3852-4246-7
HARDCOVER ISBN: 979-8-3852-4247-4
EBOOK ISBN: 979-8-3852-4248-1

VERSION NUMBER 031425

Article "Man Found Stabbed in Burned House" by Wayne Thomas, 2011. Reprinted with permission from the *Tullahoma News*.

Article "Crash Turns into Suicide Attempt" by Michael R. Moser, 2011. Reprinted with permission from the *Crossville Chronicle*.

Article "Stewart Pleads Guilty to Murder of Uncle" by Wayne Thomas, 2013.
Reprinted with permission from the *Tullahoma News*.

Except for the verse noted below, all scripture taken from the New King James Version®. Copyright © 1982 by Thomas Nelson. Used by permission. All rights reserved.

Exception: Reference to 1 Chronicles 16:22 in chapter 10 of this book.

For Travis, Jacob, and HannahGrace

May you never forget the incredible man your Papa was and even more so God's amazing, unfailing power and mercy even in the midst of tragedy.

"Watch, stand fast in the faith, be brave, be strong. Let all that you do be done with love."

1 Corinthians 16:13–14

Contents

Acknowledgments | IX
Preface | XIII
Chapter One | 1
Chapter Two | 5
Chapter Three | 10
Chapter Four | 15
Chapter Five | 20
Chapter Six | 24
Chapter Seven | 30
Dreams—First Dream | 33
Chapter Eight | 39
Chapter Nine | 44
Chapter Ten | 48
Chapter Eleven | 52
Chapter Twelve | 57
Chapter Thirteen | 62
Chapter Fourteen | 67
Dreams—Second Dream | 70
Chapter Fifteen | 77
Chapter Sixteen | 82
Chapter Seventeen | 86
Chapter Eighteen | 93
Chapter Nineteen | 96
Chapter Twenty | 103
Dreams—Third Dream | 106
Photos | 115
News Articles | 121

Acknowledgments

Writing this book and going through the processes to have it published has been quite an experience for me, and if it were not for God, of course, this story would not exist. So first and foremost I give due credit and my gratitude to God, who called upon me to be a part of all this from that midnight prayer all the way to the last page. This story is His; He just allowed me to be an intimate witness of His power and mercy. With God's guidance, I was able to put into words what transpired throughout this incredibly difficult yet beautiful time. May You, Lord, be honored in the ways You so rightly deserve.

Next in line standing strong is Kathy Taylor-Aguirre, my mama. My love and sincere appreciation pours out to you. Thank you for staying true to who you are throughout this time and always, and for "showing what for" when needed to those who needed it. You are a blessing to me beyond words.

My dear children, Travis Clay, Jacob Aaron, and Hannah-Grace, I love you all so very much. Thank you for strapping yourselves in with me during this ride. Your support and patience with me has been huge. Hold tight to God.

Adria Vaughan, my extremely talented editor and cherished friend, to say thank you is not enough. I've learned a lot from you, and not just writing business, as I am sure all who are fortunate enough to meet you do. God is surely saying to you, "Well done, my good and faithful servant." Bless you and thank you for all you've done for me. It's been an honor to work with you.

ACKNOWLEDGMENTS

Matthew Wimer, the very patient managing editor who kindly answered all my questions through this publishing process. Sir, I am so extremely grateful to you and honored that you were willing to see the heart of this story and the importance of it being told. Thank you for all your help and guidance. May God bless you in all you do.

Amber Gariety, my beautiful cousin, you have been my friend since childhood and I am truly thankful for you. I am proud of all your many accomplishments and talents and so have respected your support, cheering on's, and promptings to dig deeper and see the whole picture. Thank you.

Renee Schuster, to even write your name makes me smile. You were the first person to read my story, to have ever really even seen it. I am so grateful it was you. I love you and appreciate all you do for me.

Out of the twelve disciples, Lynda Peters would be John, whom Jesus loved. I handed you a huge pile of handwritten heartache, and you beautifully typed it all out. Beautiful inside and out is what you are. Thank you for sharing your skills with me, not to mention your patience and encouragement to me and for this story.

Miss Shelby Olsen, how precious you are. You are a force in this world, making a difference in people's lives all around you. Thank you for the help you've given me with this story and for your tremendous support. Truly I am grateful for you and all you do.

Like a super hero, Holly Britton gracefully but powerfully swooped in to save the day when I somehow turned my perfectly typed manuscript into a formatted nightmare. You knew just what to do and generously spent much time and effort fixing my fiasco. Thank you for all the years of wisdom and encouragement that you have given to this family. I do appreciate you and your lovely family!

To the highly accomplished writer and author, Frank Smart, I give you my sincere appreciation and respect. Your knowledge, guidance, and encouragement to me, and even your pushing for me to keep moving forward with this book, have been invaluable. I am grateful to know you and call you friend.

Then, there is Mike Wiedmeier, who has been a constant source of support, encouragement, and hope for me in writing this story and getting it published. You never gave up and helped me not to, either. I do sincerely thank you for all you've done for me.

Now to each and every one of you, family and friends alike, who have read my earliest version of *The Final Word*, I give my deepest appreciation to you. This story is so personal, and I was afraid to share it, to expose my heart to the world, or to even just those around me. Each of you, each in your own way, gave me important feedback and let me know how this story ministered to you. You helped in giving me the courage to be more willing to share this story and to see its importance. I am so very grateful to you all.

Preface

WHAT IF GOD, ACTUALLY God Almighty Himself, asked you if you would be thankful no matter what? Could you say yes? Without knowing the circumstances, would you be able to give an answer? Would your answer be instant, or would you need time to reason it through?

Late one night God did ask me this very question, and I answered.

Chapter One

I BOLTED AWAKE OUT of a deep sleep during the night of February 12, 2011, with an overwhelming feeling of urgency to pray for my dad. This was not something I could ignore. So, I quickly sat up in bed and began to call out to God on Dad's behalf, even though I had no idea what it was that I was supposed to be praying about. What could be happening to my father at this moment that would warrant this demand of God's attention?

Maybe he was having some sort of medical emergency? I personally know of God's healing power, so I prayed, asking God to heal my dad's body of whatever may be going on that shouldn't be. After those words were spoken, I knew Dad's health wasn't the reason I was woken up to pray.

I began again, praying now for whatever I could think of, hoping I would get it right. I was throwing out lines baited with bits of everything, trying to feel for the one that would hook into the purpose of God's prompting. Things like, that my dad would know how much he was loved and needed, that he would be happy. Praying my family and I would be able to rent a bigger house so Dad could have his own room, since he spent more time off at my house than at his own. Praying over his trucking business as an owner-operator. Safety while he drove, his finances—no, none of these things was it.

What is it, God?

His soul. It was for my dad's very soul I then knew I was to pray for.

The Final Word

Dad had told me several times over the years that he absolutely knew God was real—"more than most others," he would say—and I knew that came about from different miraculous experiences and "dealin's" he'd had over his lifetime with God. But at this moment, with such an intense feeling of needing to pray for him, those assurances of his did not settle the issue for me. Knowing that God is real is not enough to save your soul; for even the devil and his demons have known that God is real, long before we ever did, yet still their destiny is sealed for eternal damnation.

Yes, I knew my dad believed in God. And for the previous seventeen years I had watched him willingly be transformed into more of the man he was created to be. For those of us who had seen and had personally lived out the painful consequences that resulted from his, at times, unrestrained choices that often seemed to have no rhyme or reason, it could be hard to believe him to be a changed man. This would be true also for those who had only heard the stories. But his transformation was real, and he did willingly and humbly (the best a man such as himself could) allow it to happen. It was a process that took time, with many ups and downs, but it did happen. I can testify to the truth of this and proudly I do. Throughout this time I had walked beside my dad, and we learned and changed together.

But still, yes, even with all of that, this undeniable prompting to pray for Dad caused me to worry he had not fully given his heart to Jesus. I knew my dad confessed that God was the reason he was alive, that He was his healer. *But, does Junior Taylor, my Dad, know Jesus as the Savior of his soul, the Lord of his life?* This weak questioning of mine will boldly become clear to me before this story is through. Forgive me.

Once I knew what to pray for, I felt my spirit rise up and strengthen. *There aren't no hindrances between God and me now,* I thought. The line hooked onto what it had intended to and with the target held fast I was able to zero in on praying: if for some reason my dad truly did not know Jesus as the only one who could save his soul, that he would now want to. That he would know how much he was loved by God, and that he really could be completely

Chapter One

forgiven, with nothing left within him untouched—because at times he felt he could never truly be forgiven. I prayed, pleading with God, that my dad would reach out to Him with an honest desire, call out His name, and finally know, because of God's mercy, he was worthy to receive all our Lord had for him.

Suddenly, something changed. There was a very noticeable shift within me; it felt as though there was a sharp jerk aiming my focus toward a new direction. The spotlight was moving away from what I thought had been the sole purpose of this encounter tonight. The pressure driving me in what I felt I needed to do or say on my dad's behalf subsided. I did not bring this meeting to order, nor did I prepare its agenda. God was in charge, and He came with his own plans drawn up. There, in the pitch-black darkness of my small, shabby bedroom, as I was still sitting upright in the middle of my side of our bed, next to my surprisingly sleeping, unaware husband, God revealed the fate of my dad to me. Gently but firmly God told me Dad's life here on Earth would soon be over. From the way I felt, I understood God's announcement informing me my dad was to die was not open for discussion. He was resolute in what was to be. God is the author and finisher of our faith and lives. I know Jesus holds the key to the book of life, but still, this was serious, and it was my dad, so bull-headed me, I quickly, desperately (like it would make a difference) tried to change God's mind. I did not know how soon his end would come, but I wanted to make sure my dad was ready, so again I prayed for the salvation of his soul.

Then, right in the midst of it, with the abruptness of a slammed door, God interrupted me. Very clearly, very matter-of-fact, but softly, quietly, my God asked me out loud, "Would you be thankful no matter what?" I did not need time to think this question through. Without hesitation my spirit answered back, "Yes, God, no matter what I will be thankful." I repeated this now out loud, again, and then again, more intensely each time.

This was not a casual question God just asked me. And absolutely it was the Almighty Himself who asked. Strangely, though only moments ago God had confided in me that Dad's life was coming to an end, I was not afraid for him. I didn't want my dad to die, but I was not afraid for him because I knew my prayers were heard. Jesus was there with Dad now. And because of who God is I was able to lie back down and go to sleep. I think too I could sleep because of the surety I felt in believing that who my dad was and his strength would always protect him from the dangers of this world.

Even so, I wonder now if I would have felt the same way had I known how he would die. Would my prayers have been different? Could I have stopped the evils that were lurking beyond my sight? Would I have told my dad? All the unknowns and what ifs can be cruel.

I was the one to be called upon in the night for reasons I do not know and compelled to follow my God through places I could never have imagined. I would become a part of something so overwhelmingly grotesque and foul but, yet, laden with such beauty and power that I could not look away.

You will shortly see, as our story unfolds, that it is filled with the words "I" and "me." They were not written to satisfy a self-centered thirst, but only because of my first-hand experience in what God has graciously allowed me to join Him in. This story is ultimately His, so it being filled with so much of myself has made the process of writing and sharing it difficult for me. But all who were involved here have their own tales to tell, and this one is mine.

Chapter Two

I awoke that Sunday morning, February 13th, with the night's prayer event still fresh in my mind and thinking how strange it all was. What was made known to me about Dad was heavy on my heart, and so was God's question to me. Whispering, I prayed, asking God not to let my dad suffer in his passing. And again I told Him that I would be thankful no matter what.

I needed to get up and get ready for church, but instead, I just sat there in my cold room on the edge of my bed for a few more minutes. In this small, little-house-on-the-prairie look-of-a-house, it was hard to have any privacy. But I needed to have a moment here, while I was alone, to think about what had happened. Last night, all that was said and done happened for a reason, but what? And what was I meant to do with it? I was wondering if I somehow missed an important part of the message, or did God fail to mention the details of exactly how soon or what was to be the cause of Dad leaving us? But no matter what was to come, I absolutely knew God heard my prayers last night—of course He did—and so I believed He and my dad worked out what needed to be between them. This probably sounds like I was very nonchalant about what God had revealed to me, or that I didn't care about my dad or his life. I did care! I loved him very much. Dad meant the world to me. Maybe that's why God didn't tell me how my dad would die. For I believe if God had given me all the details of what lay ahead, I would have furiously fought like all get out to shove God out of the way in order to save him, destroying what was meant to be that spanned out far beyond just this instance.

I was up now, making sure the kids—Travis, Jacob, and HannahGrace—were getting ready for church, resisting my heart's gravitational pull toward the phone to call Dad. I wanted to hear how he was this morning, what had happened between him and God last night. But I would have to wait until after church.

My life was not my own, and what I needed or wanted was rarely considered in my marriage. I wanted to call my dad right then, to hear his voice, to talk to him about what had happened last night. I wanted him to know I prayed for him and that no matter what God would be there with him (I strongly felt God would not leave him to face his fate alone). Regrettably, instead, I did what was required, demanded, of me. For my husband ruled my life and our family with a strong, unpredictable presence and a heavy hand. There was not much of anything that I had any say-so over.

When church was over we came straight home, and I was to make lunch for everyone. I had told no one of anything that had happened during the night or what was said. I held it all privately, safely in my heart, protecting such a beautiful gift from the harshness of my life. It would be a long time before I told anyone.

I knew I would have to work fast to get all I had to done so I could call Dad before it got much later.

Since I awoke that morning I was anxious to hear how the Creator of heaven and earth reached down last night and touched my dad's heart and soul, ministering to him, maybe even as I was praying for him. I was curious to know how he was spending his time today. Did he look or feel different? Did the world seem different to him, as though he were seeing it in a new light? Was he filled with a sense of freedom and joy, or was he sad, unsure of where to go, how to step forward from what I was imagining might have happened to him in the presence of God? Had He revealed to my dad the fact that his life would end soon or was it that only I knew?

Finally my chores were all done. I had even quickly put together a special Valentine's treat for the kids, and after putting their cake into the oven I excitedly took off my apron so I could sit and

Chapter Two

talk with my dad. As I was hanging my apron up, the telephone suddenly rang.

"Good, maybe it's Dad," I thought; but it wasn't. It was Mrs. Montgomery from the Tullahoma church we attended as a family for so many years in Tennessee before moving to California. She said she was calling me because she had heard over the emergency scanner that my dad's house was on fire.

Mrs. Montgomery was always someone people could count on for help. I thanked her for calling me, then I hung up the phone. While I dialed my dad's cell phone number, I told my husband and the kids what Mrs. Montgomery just said. As the phone was ringing, I said a quick prayer for God to take care of Dad.

Dad didn't answer his phone, so I called again. Then again a third time. Still no answer. I was really beginning to worry, but then I thought, *Well, maybe he was a-tryin' to call me, but I was keepin' the line busy?* So, I hung up my end of the line and waited for Dad to call me.

The kids were now around me, asking if their Papa was all right. I told them calmly, "I'm not sure yet, but I'm workin' on tryin' to find out." It'd been more than five minutes that had gone by, which I thought was long enough for Dad to have called me. So I quickly tried calling him again, hoping this time he'd pick up and I'd hear his voice. But again, no answer. *Gee whiz!* With a frustrated sigh, I thought, *Alright, Junior Taylor, where ya at?* I could feel I already knew, but I purposely ignored that thought. It was like if I didn't make eye contact with it or acknowledge this realization, it wouldn't be true. I didn't want it to be true, not so soon.

Now I knew it was time to call my mom. *Plus*, I thought hopefully, *Dad may have called her between my calls to him.* So, I called her and asked her if she'd heard from Dad today. Mom told me no, she hadn't, and asked why. I then told her how Mrs. Montgomery had called me just a bit ago to tell me that she heard on the scanner that Dad's house was on fire. I told her how I'd been calling since, but he wasn't answering.

Mom replied, "Well, I'm sure he's okay," but she also told me to try calling him again.

She was calm, but I could tell by her voice she was concerned. I'm sure a big reason why she was not overly concerned just yet was because, of all people, my mama was the one to know that my dad was someone who could survive and beat the odds when others thought there'd be no chance. There are so many instances that have happened throughout Dad's life that would prove the point of his tremendous strength and determination. Here's one such example of a story Mom has told me that happened when we all lived in Oregon, when my brother and I were young. This story involves her, Dad, and two others—Mom's older sister and their pregnant friend. It was early spring, and they were all in a raft together going down the icy Rogue River—maybe not a good idea.

All was fine, Mom said, until those snowmelt waters quickly went from a seemingly safe, manageable current into a raging, angry nightmare that was hell-bent on pulling whatever was within its banks over a very large, unforeseen waterfall up ahead. The raft and its four-man crew got pinned against the gnarled, upturned roots of a fallen tree that was in the middle of the river. The raft then flipped, dumping all four people into the deep, freezing waters. Against the voluminous force of the river's current that was being sucked down the waterfall, my mom says Dad was able to single-handedly right the raft and put all three ladies into it. He then got himself in and fought using the only oar that wasn't lost to make it to shore. His only concern was for his passengers, who he was finally able to get to land safely before they went over the waterfall. She told me dad was calm and quiet throughout it all, but tried to encourage her and the other two women, and even made them laugh, which I am not surprised by. And I should mention, it was a cold and rainy day. Why they went rafting on such a day, I have no idea.

I've personally also seen him pull off amazing feats just by being who he is, with no drama or thought of himself in the act. No matter how challenging or ugly the circumstance, my dad would sincerely tell me that he had nothing to complain about because he was blessed. And he was. And so am I, for both my parents are extraordinary, each in their own way.

Chapter Two

Dad left here a little less than two weeks before this day, February 13th, that set in motion events that will forever be etched in my mind and heart.

Chapter Three

My dad, along with many of our relatives, had told me often how much he and I were alike. I am thankful for this but know I could never measure up to the person my dad was. I was so thankful for him. I needed my dad in my life and am grateful for the time he gave and sincerely spent with me. Being with him was calming to me because of that sense of likeness between one another; there's peace that comes from understanding each other's ways and mind. For the kids and I, there was safety and a feeling of normalcy when Dad was by our side, even if it could only be on the surface. He didn't know what our world was like when he drove away, but whenever we were with him, he was our refuge, and we held on to him tight.

When Dad's recent visit had come to an end and it was time for him to leave, we took him to his work tractor and trailer parked not far from where we lived off Highway 108. Dad drove truck; that is what he had done to earn a living his entire adult life beginning at seventeen years old while in the United States Army.

Before we left the house, Dad told me that he'd lined up a load that was going to be the load of all loads, pay-wise, and I could tell he thought he was pretty clever for setting these up. They were three separate pickups here in the West, not far from each other, and all of them were to be delivered back East as one load, along the same route. Two were of military heavy equipment and the third was a large roll of metal coils for a factory. He carefully calculated the lengths and weights of each so to fit all together on his extra-long flatbed trailer.

Chapter Three

"Pretty handy you're good at math, huh?" I said.

"Yeah, where do ya reckon you got your brains from?" he said with a wink, teasing.

My dad was a man of many talents. He was ingenious in many ways, and so funny. He was an incredibly gifted mechanic, had raced cars, learned to fly, broke horses—he taught me to ride at an early age and how to handle and care for animals of all sorts. He was adventurous, and there wasn't much my dad was afraid of or afraid to try. So, putting that together with his determination and strength, not to mention that charm of his, he would become unstoppable at times. This helped him succeed and overcome much in his life, but there were times these traits led him to trouble, for determination down a path you ought not be on often becomes a curse and no longer an asset.

As I leaned against our van I watched Dad climb up into his truck to start the engine and toss his bag onto the bunk behind him. He then climbed down to walk all around the tractor and trailer, checking lights and hitting the tires. When he was done, Dad walked up to my husband to shake his hand, then he went over to where the kids stood waiting to say goodbye. One by one their Papa cupped each of his grandchildren's faces in his large hands and kissed them on the tops of their heads. He then told them he'd be back in the spring with his fishin' pole.

I walked over with Dad to his truck and told him how glad I was for his visits and that he was always welcome to stay with us. He said that he had to go, but, as he was hugging me, he seemed like he didn't want to leave. When I told my dad that I loved him, he then let go, ruffled the top of my head, gave me a wink, then turned around and climbed up into his truck to head out.

I went back to our vehicle—my husband and the kids were already inside—but I didn't get in just yet. To me there is nothin' like the sound of an idlin' truck and the smell of diesel in the cool of the morning. Then to hear the release of the air brakes and see the slow, shaky rumble of the tractor as the tires begin to roll forward.

This scene has been a part of my life as far back as I can remember. It was my mom, then, who was driving Dad to his truck, when it wasn't parked at our house, bringing us kids with her in the early morning hours. He would hug my brother and me, ruffle our hair, then hold my mom in his arms and kiss her goodbye, saying he'd see us all soon.

These were happy memories, and sad ones, too. I felt the same in that moment just like all those other times in the past as I watched him pull out onto the highway.

When I got into the van, I told my husband it felt like Dad didn't want to go. He seemed to look at us all as though he would never see us again. My husband agreed.

I thought of that now, bringing myself back into the present situation. As I was pacing on the front porch in the chill of the afternoon, I tried Dad's number again. Still no answer. I needed to know if my dad was all right. Who could I call? I went inside and decided to call my brother, even though I didn't think he knew anything about what was going on.

My brother, to my frustration and Dad's disappointment and hurt, was not involved in much of our father's life, nor even seemed to care much about it. My brother and his family lived only a little more than a block from Dad. You would think it would be easy for any of them to stay connected with him, but he was never high enough on their list of priorities. Between working and his time with me, Dad wasn't home much, but still, my brother or his family could have reached out to our father beyond just when they wanted something from him, like how others treated him.

Even through all of his failures and struggles, my dad, Junior Taylor, made something out of his life he could be proud of. I am proud of him. He was successful, yet humble. There were some who had seen my dad only as a means to get the things they wanted. Greedily and disrespectfully they took, feeling somehow entitled to his heart, his earnings, his possessions. They demanded things from him they had no right to have.

When I got Brother on the phone, I told him what I had heard and that I had not been able to get ahold of Dad. Of course, I was not surprised that he didn't know what was going on, but with news

Chapter Three

like this, I was surprised that he wasn't even concerned about it or interested in going over to Dad's to check on him. He seemed to only care about the movie he was watching. I needed to know if he was all right, so I repeatedly asked my brother to go to Dad's place for me. I angrily demanded that he get himself on over there and tell me what was happening. Finally, he agreed.

My brother told me that he would call me on his cell phone when he got there. *His house isn't far, so it shouldn't take long now to find out what's happened*, I thought. I went outside again and stood near the front door on the top step of a long, multi-tiered set of stairs, checking to see if, by chance, there had been any messages left on my phone's voicemail while I waited. There were none.

"Where's Dad?" I asked God. I wanted to hear an answer different from where I already felt he was. I had been calm so far and not overly worried, but thinking of this made me feel afraid of what was coming. Outside, waiting for the phone to ring, I thought about how me not being someone quick to panic or become overwhelmed was a good thing. A steady spirit is important, and little did I know I was going to need it.

The call back from my brother was taking longer than I thought it should. It's hard being beyond the reach of something you feel you should be taking care of. It was me who my dad relied on. My heart ached at the thought of him needing me now, and I felt useless to him just standing here, waiting. I always knew what to do or who needed to be called when taking care of my dad or the things in his life. Never had I needed to ask or go through someone else before I did what needed to be done. Whatever it was, I took care of it! But this time I was waiting for news to be brought to me. I didn't like it. God is God and I am not, so I needed to take a breath and be patient.

Finally, the phone rang. I quickly looked at the caller ID to see if it was my dad's number. It wasn't. It was my brother who told me that our dad's house really was on fire and that Dad was nowhere to be seen, even though his work truck and personal vehicles were all there.

Lots of activity was already going on when my brother and his family got there. The police and fire departments were there, along with a couple family members, curious friends, and nearby neighbors. I was not the only one trying to find out what was going on.

My initial question of needing to know where Dad was could not be answered right then. Within the hour that mystery would be solved, and from there many new questions would emerge.

For the rest of that afternoon and late into the evening my brother and his wife kept me informed as the events unfolded, even though they were having a hard time there in the midst of it. Some of those new questions would be answered that night, but so many would not be solved for a very long time. This had to be the reason I needed to pray for Dad last night. God knew what was going to happen, and He was there now. I must not forget this. As sudden and sad as it was to hear from Him that my dad was going to die, God was unbelievably kind to have told me, and I am so very appreciative for such a gift. But then, there was also His question to me. Was that for this same reason too?

Chapter Four

Dad lived on the East side of town, the wrong side of the tracks, if you will, as that's where our family is from and who we are. There, on an extra-large, very pretty, downward-sloping corner lot, heading outside of town toward Manchester, is where his eighteen-foot-wide, simple but respectable mobile home sat. It had a large, detached shop next to it that held all of his mechanican' stuff, as I called it, and a long pull-through driveway that made for easy comin' and goin's for his truck, since he was so near the highway. Dad took a lot of pride in keeping his place looking nice and well-cared for. This is from where smoke was seen coming out, which was reported to the Tullahoma Fire Department by a kind neighbor in the early afternoon of February 13th.

A lot of thick black smoke was rolling out of what we used as the front door, which stepped down onto the porch, and from many of the windows when the fire department arrived.

The firefighters quickly got busy and, once inside, they were able to extinguish the flames. The fire itself was just in the living room, but there was severe heat and smoke damage throughout the whole house. This was because, as we later learned, the fire was started with gasoline.

With the fire now out, the smoke cleared enough to reveal to the firefighters that this situation was more than a mere house fire. They called the Tullahoma Police Department to the scene. Inside the house, lying face up on the living room floor, was my dad's body. It was obvious to the officers that he had not died as a result of the fire or of natural causes, either. It was not by flames his body was destroyed. From this discovery, other law enforcement agencies were called in to assist with the investigative processes.

We, as a family, were given information only a piece at a time throughout that evening. At first, we were only told that somebody was found in the house. Even though we were not told who it was or the person's condition, I knew right then that the person was obviously my dad and he was no longer alive. I knew because God had just come to me in the coldest, darkest hours of the night to ready me for this news. It did not take long for this early warning to be confirmed.

I knew my dad had died, but I didn't know how. I hoped it had not been a struggle for him and that he hadn't suffered in his passing. A scenario began to form in my mind to explain what had happened. I thought, "Well maybe he sadly had a heart attack while smoking and a fire was started from a dropped cigarette?" This was unlikely, because Dad was not one to smoke in his house, but I was trying to come up with something.

With calls now coming in from several different people, I could tell rumors were quickly being weaved from the few threads of truth. The ever-growing rumors soon became a huge tangled mess that spread out in all directions. These lies and all the ones to come were so very frustrating and hurtful. The truth was bad enough. Why did some people think they needed to add to it?

By about eight o'clock that night, enough facts had come in (from the officers themselves) that I knew it was time to go. My dad, my dear father, had been robbed and brutally murdered in his home which was then set on fire to cover up the crime. For the last couple of hours I had tried to think of causes for Dad's death and reason it through. But this was nothing like what I had thought of and there was no way to make sense of it.

How could this have happened? Men feared my dad; there was just something notable about him that commanded respect. I'd seen here and there over the years people who must have thought he needed to be taken down a notch or two, but every time it was they who were quickly put down in one way or another. He had never been robbed or beaten up at truck stops or work yards as others have been. This is hard to explain, but if you knew my dad, you'd understand. It was clear to me that the only way he could have been murdered was by God allowing it to happen. God does not create the sin and hatred that runs rampant in this world, but He does at times allow it for reasons that are not for us to understand.

My mom had now called her family to her and, like the good Mama she is, she wanted to gather us all up under the protection and comfort of her wings. My husband, with surprisingly gentle yet steady direction, helped focus the children and me in order to get ourselves and our household ready to go.

There was no supper for anyone that night. The oven had been turned off hours ago, but that cake meant to be a special Valentine's treat was forgotten and ended up staying in the oven for over a couple weeks. I cancelled my scheduled work plans—all previously made plans no longer mattered. My children were all being homeschooled by me. My brain seemed far away, and I was having a hard time in this moment ordering or following through with my thoughts, but still the kids not falling behind in their studies stood out enough to me for me to put together, the best I could, modified versions of their lessons to take with us. God was adjusting all of our plans; He was carving out a new path I was to take.

Our first steps were to spend the night together at Mom's house and then leave, hopefully, first thing in the morning for Tennessee. We left our home in silence that dark and snowy night, heartbroken, knowing that the unthinkable was now real.

I was warned by God that my dad was going to die, but in such a gruesome way and so soon, how could this actually be true? Two weeks ago he was with me, he was safe. During his visit, Dad would relax and close the door to the world. In the innocence of play there was silliness, and his youth was restored in snowball fights and him diving on top of Travis and Jacob as they sped past him, sledding down the steep road in front of our house. Dad would laugh as he saved Miss Grace from her brothers who wanted to push her into the several-feet-deep snow. Inside our odd, blue house that was tucked back up on a wooded lot in the mountains, my Dad would stretch his long, six-foot-two body out on the living room floor in front of the warmth of the wood stove as the kids and I, and the dog too, played games with him, and he would tell us stories. We took up the entire living room floor area, but my husband knew better than to show his annoyance of this in front of Junior Taylor. I loved listening to my dad, the sound of his deep Southern voice, his genuine, full laughter, watching all of his animated expressions with those words and looks that are uniquely his.

Dad was here for more than a week, and on one of those days, he, my Uncle Jeff, and all of us went higher up the mountain to sled at a place called Little Sweden.

Uncle Jeff was my dad's beloved, longtime friend. They had met and become friends while in the Army when they both were stationed in Germany, where I was born. It was there my uncle also met my mom's younger sister, Linda, whom he later married. My Aunt Linda had come, only being sixteen, all the way to Germany to help my poor mama with her set of "Irish twins." I was a bit early, so my brother was only ten months old when I was born there, in Landstuhl, at the old military hospital. Dear Aunt Linda was a godsend to our mother, who is eternally grateful, as you can imagine, for the help her sister willingly gave during that year she was there.

Aunt Linda and our soon-to-be uncle left Germany while my family stayed awhile more before being sent to the next base where my dad continued his duties as a driver in the transportation department. Dad was in the military for six years. We did not always live near my aunt and uncle, but my brother's and my bonds and love for both of them have never faded.

After our day in the snow, we all came back to my house to eat a hot bowl of homemade beans and cornbread that I had made. While we all sat around the table, I listened to my dad and uncle tease each other about who was more of a dummy, as they said, and to their stories as they reminisced about some of their adventures together. These usually involved cars or trucks, my dad's uncommon strength and the fights he got into, and, of course, stories about my mom and animals. Everyone laughed, listened, and watched, soaking this treasured time in. It was good to be together. A lot was shared in that week, as was in all his visits here with us since we'd moved from Tennessee. There would be no more visits, no new memories made with my dad, only the old ones to hold on to.

Chapter Five

THE MORNING COULD NOT come fast enough for me. My mom and all of us stayed up late into the night, huddled together, whispering in the darkness of her living room. It was as if speaking fully out loud would make the horrors of what had happened actually real and give power to the evil that shattered our world that day. We were fully aware of the facts that were given to us so far, but we spoke cautiously of them. I heard what was being spoken, but my thoughts were on figuring out a way for me to get to Tennessee by tomorrow. My dad was actually no longer there, I knew this, but I still couldn't help feeling that I needed to be there with him, to be there for him.

For several years Dad had been letting me know that he wanted me to take care of all his final business when he died. Two weeks prior, while at my house, Dad again told me this final-business stuff of his, just in more detail than usual. I was given codes, keys; he told me where I would find things that would be important for me to have and use, along with having me write down any personal information of his that I did not already have. He gave me the names of his attorneys and what business of his they were in charge of. It was not only business or financial matters that my dad made sure I knew, but when it was just he and I, Dad also poured out matters of his heart that he obviously felt led to share with me. There wasn't much by this point in my life that I didn't already know. I've had the keys to my dad's heart for a long time now. One of the keys on that priceless ring was of me knowing which questions to ask. Asking the right questions unlocked those

Chapter Five

hidden away doors of his heart. Often I would open those doors and he would then freely tell me anything and everything. I thank God my dad trusted me—with his life and heart. Because of that trust, Dad told me that whatever it was that had to be done, he knew I would take care of it for him. This time, when I said that I would, I could see in his eyes that he knew I meant it, and he was relieved. Did he know somehow that his life was about to end? No, it wasn't that his life was about to end—it was to be violently taken from him!

It was difficult putting our plan together with so many different ideas going back and forth. Yes, I had to get to Tennessee. I had made a promise, but I was not the only one huddled there in our circle that night who loved Dad. We all wanted to go.

My brother was in Tennessee, and my mom wanted to be there for him with love and support like she was for me now. Mom had been Dad's wife. She is the mother of his children. She had a right to be there. My parents did end up divorcing while my brother and I were young, but they still cared about one another. They were only really just teenagers when they married, and their marriage had been a whirlwind of faraway adventures, passion, excitement, and love from beginning to end. But it was also filled with an incredible amount of heartache and loss as a result of Dad's self-destructive behaviors and choices. Yet, my parents had such a unique and interesting life together in their ten years of marriage, with their children in tow. I have many memories of them together and of their love for one another that I cherish and never want to forget and, too, some that make me want to cry. It makes me smile to remember Mom sitting on Dad's lap, and he'd say funny things, making her laugh. Then he'd wink at us kids—her laughter was his prize. So was my mother's beauty, inside and out. She was, and still is today, so very beautiful, and you could see Dad knew that by the way he looked at her, because her beauty goes far deeper than just her looks. My incredible mom put up with a lot and really did do her best to hold us all together. My dad's love and efforts, how he felt, all he did for his wife and children, his desire for our family, was all genuine and can't be discounted, but as the saying goes, "The spirit indeed is willing, but the flesh is weak" (Matt 26:41). Numerous times over the years, dad expressed how deeply he regretted what he had put his young wife through, and often he would tell me, "Through it all, your mother has been and ever will be the only woman I have ever loved."

This was, once again, told to me by him when he came to visit us here just recently. Dad was even more adamant about making sure I knew the love he'd always had for my mama—if I hadn't known by now, I'd obviously have had a real understanding issue going on. I told him then, while we were alone, outside on my snow-covered porch, that I knew he loved her and how much it meant to me that he did. I also told him I hoped he knew, too, how much I loved him.

My children loved my dad, their Papa, very much, and they were the joy of his life, even still at the ages of 15, 13, and 10. I wanted the kids to go. I needed them to go. Saying Travis, Jacob, and Grace were a huge part of my life is an understatement. They had been by my side through so many ugly, despairing times. Our bonds and my love for them were strong. I knew I would need them. We would all need each other in the days to come. My husband said he also wanted to go.

Who would go was not the only factor to be decided that night. It was also the when and how that had to be sorted through. I was adamant that I had to leave in the morning by whatever means I could, making that very clear. It was the timing that was a problem for my mom; and for us, as usual, it was the very limited amount of money.

Finally, after weeding through all the issues, our plan was made. My husband and I would fly out in the morning. At the end of the week, Mom would fly out to Tennessee, as my husband would be leaving from there that same day, their travel times intersecting one another. The kids would be staying with Mom along with my dog, Daisy, and even the bunny. Then, on the day she was to leave for Tennessee, the kids and critters would be dropped off at our Uncle Jeff's house, where they would be taken care of until

Chapter Five

their dad arrived that night. Uncle Jeff was my dad's friend and wanted to help, and he did as he so generously always does.

After only a few fretful hours of sleep, I was up getting ready to go. I was tired and emotionally drained. We all were, but I was anxious to get going. Soon the others were up, too. Mom would be driving us to the airport.

With a great sense of loss, I said goodbye to each of my children. My heart was torn in two. Half was left for them and the other half was for Dad, but his piece was struggling, barely able to beat for fear of what lay ahead east of the Mississippi. I didn't want to leave the kids behind. I wanted them with me, but we couldn't afford for all of them to go, and it was best not to separate the kids. The relationships they had with one another would be an important source for them to draw strength and comfort from.

And so we left, and I did not know when I would return. I prayed my children would forgive me and that our God would stand protectively by their side, being all they each needed in their own grief and fears. As their mother I wanted to be the one to hold and comfort them, helping them to hold fast so as not to be lost in this storm, but I had to let go and trust God to step in and be for my children far more than I ever could be.

So now the opening scene has been laid before you, which began with a midnight prayer and ended with the thrust of the engines lifting the jet off the runway, pushing me forward.

I cannot turn back.

Chapter Six

My husband and I arrived in Tullahoma late that night, having taken a taxi all the way from the Nashville airport. Only a few hours later it was daybreak, and I was up taking a shower. As I sat on the bed finishing combing out my wet hair, our former pastor, Joe, arrived to lend us one of his cars. All those years attending that church, I had regularly witnessed the steadfast spirit of our generous and faithful pastor. And even now, after being gone five years, I saw this man was still true to who he was.

As a child, I lived in several places, and for a time Tullahoma was one of those places, and I made many returning visits. When I turned seventeen, I moved back and stayed late into my thirtieth year. This town, and its surrounding areas, has been my home physically and within my heart. Here is where I met God; I graduated high school here, got married and had all my babies. I grew up here and learned of life, experiencing both the good and the bad. I no longer live in Tennessee, but no matter where I'm at, it will always be a part of me. That was true for my dad also; in all of his travels he never lost sight of being just a poor boy born and raised in the South.

We checked out of the motel and went straight to the police station. As my husband drove, I glanced around our borrowed vehicle and laughed to myself, seeing how this was definitely Joe's car (the different things lying about showed the busyness of his life). Before anything else was done that morning, the station had to be our first stop—I needed to hear and see the truth for myself, especially before going to what was left of my dad's house. I wanted

Chapter Six

to know the facts gathered so far before being bombarded with the speculations and rumors that had rapidly gained momentum and were running out of control. Such nonsense as: Dad was involved in a drug deal gone bad or a mafia-type crime, and other ridiculous stuff that was nothing of who my dad was. He was very much against drugs, stealing, or using and hurting people as the means to get what you want in life. These types of things made him angry; of course I knew the rumors were false.

So often, no matter my age, all the way up until I last saw him, Dad would firmly say to me, "Little Girl, I better not ever hear of you stealin' or doin' no dope." Or it'd be, "Little Girl, I best not ever catch you drinkin' alcohol"—and for sure he'd make it clear I was not to cuss, use people, or be lazy. "I'll stripe them legs," he'd say (a good switchin' is what I'd get), and I knew he'd do it, even with me being an adult, that didn't matter. Dad was serious about me treating people right and not living in ways many people did around us. When I messed up or he saw something in me he wasn't liking, Dad was quick to correct me. He expected a lot from me, while I was a kid and as an adult, and I'm thankful he loved me enough to do so. But I have been far from perfect and have disappointed and frustrated him, I'm sure, more times than I can count. Me, pregnant only a couple of weeks after graduating high school and being unmarried in this situation, was definitely a blow Dad hadn't expected or wanted. Absolutely he was angry with me, but the shame and guilt I carried with me even long after I was married and with more children, along with knowing how I disappointed him, was much worse of a punishment to me than what I got from him and others.

These accusations people were making were wrong. It's true, here in the South superstitions run deep and old wives' tales are not to be doubted. Some will make you laugh, but it's best not to if you don't wanna get slapped or be forced to take the remedy to what ails ya. So, by some, the rumors were brought about for a reason, but to me they were just hateful and could hold no water.

Waiting outside the investigator's door, I knew this was not going to be easy—probably horrific—but running out of here was not an option. Didn't I make a promise to my father that I would take care of whatever had to be done for him? Is this what God, my heavenly Father, was warning me of, preparing me for, just two nights ago? Yes, I believe it was!

The door was opened by an officer who I gladly recognized, Officer Ferrell—though he was higher ranking now, a sergeant of criminal investigations. Crossing over the threshold into his office opened up for me the path I would have to travel upon for a long time to come. Once seated inside, this confident, professional yet compassionate, investigator calmly told me all the known facts he could about how my dad died from multiple, multiple stab wounds.

Why? It was believed that the murderer's purpose was to rob my dad of the large sum of cash in his wallet that he recently withdrew (which I knew was a cheaper way for him to pay for his fuel). He had told me Saturday, when I had talked to him, that he planned on heading out very early Monday morning at 3 a.m.—this was his favorite time to leave. I had by this point been logging my dad's books and managing the ins and outs of his trucking business for many years. And it would be me who would log his last loads, putting down the final entry that was to close out the books of his career. So, a man's life ended for what? Money? This wasn't just any man, either. He was a good man, a respected man. He was my dad, and his life didn't just end—he was viciously murdered. I am struck with the truth in the words, "For the love of money is a root of all kinds of evil" (1 Tim 6:10). Greed has caused much sorrow in the world.

We continued our discussion for a while more, not only about what had happened but also about what kind of man my dad was. By what this officer and the other officials I came in contact with were telling me, it was obvious they felt Junior Taylor had left an extraordinary mark on people's lives. This was not news I didn't already know. They spoke of there being people in our town who would not have a home of their own if it were not for my dad and the weight of his word. They spoke of the stories from fellow long-haulers who had witnessed for years Dad quietly, with no explanation or expectations for him to do so, give jackets or

Chapter Six

sleeping bags to hitchhikers and those in need at truck stops. My dad never mentioned this to me or anyone else, but people saw—plus I'd always find his stash of secret mercies to the cold and lost when I'd clean his truck. There was a stack of them that I pulled out from under his bunk when I cleaned out his rig for the final time. I donated the jackets and sleeping bags to a shelter. His unspoken deeds were more than the spoken.

While we were there Sergeant Ferrell even gave us some details regarding the capture of the murderer northeast off of Interstate 40, a few hours after his unimaginable acts of evil. This man was not a stranger to me; he was a second cousin to Dad and just three years older than I. I knew him, and all his many siblings, well. Never had I imagined that this cousin of ours would one day be a murderer. Yet, when the police officers told me that it was Stephen Stewart who had killed my dad, strangely I was not surprised at all.

Before we left, the officer had noticed me looking at a photocopied picture of my dad's driver's license picture on his desk. With a kind smile Sergeant Ferrell got out his scissors, cut that out, and handed it to me.

This first week was the beginning of the flurry of responsibilities I was handed the keys to. I felt as though, in the midst of this whirlwind, I was slowly groping my way along this path all alone through a cold, thick fog, often shaking uncontrollably from that cold I felt. A funeral had to be planned, even though my dad's body was sent to Nashville for the required autopsy to be conducted by the state. There were police officers to be met with, as well as attorneys, bankers, the trucking company my dad was leased to, and the most stressful part was dealing with the irrational demands unmercifully and relentlessly pushed on me by my brother and many others in our family. There were people scattered about in all directions who hounded me to solve the odd personal or legal problems they were having, even though they were often angry at me. Our family has quite a history of mystery and a lot of dealin's in questionable activity that took root during the Civil War and were allowed to thrive. That poisonous weed is still abundantly producing fruit to this day. So, even though this unjustifiable crime crossed all lines of morality, I was still pressured to not bring charges against the murderer because we were family. The list was long of what I had to do and what was expected of me at both ends of the country, and that list would only continue to grow.

Looking back, I can clearly see now that, as I was walking through that fog, I was not totally alone. God, of course, was with me. He had been with me since He woke me up the night before my dad's life was stolen away.

It was God who was giving me the strength and wisdom to handle what I had to, to make the decisions that had to be made, and to deal with the outrageous demands and anger that were being shoved at me. Thankfully, there was also some help from various individuals—like from our former pastor in Tullahoma and his wife; from a dear woman from that church who let my husband and I, then my mom and I, stay at her house; there was a good friend of my dad's who came to be a pallbearer for my dad, even though he had said goodbye to his own father only days earlier; and then from a few special family members. There was also, of course, the invaluable help and support from my mama and kids. My husband? Well, he did what he thought he should.

I ended up being gone from my home and children for a month. There was so much I had to get done right away and much more that had to be put into motion—work I would be continuing with for a long time to come. My mom and I ended up driving my dad's Ford pickup home to California. It was a comfort to be driving his truck. I could smell him in it and see things of him, like a motor grease handprint on the interior above the driver's side door. I was glad to have it in many ways, and I still am today.

Both my mama and I were exhausted physically and emotionally after all that had happened during that past month, but still, we were able to laugh and see some of the beauty around us. To still be able to see some good in life and people, to be able to laugh still, even in the midst of unbelievable ugliness and heartache, was a trait both my parents had, and that gift was passed on to myself and a bit to my children. Not all people have this gift. We are fortunate.

A little after midnight, after that trip, my mom and I said our goodbyes with sadness in our hearts, but with eyes that flashed sparks of God's greatness. At the end of our journey, I left her safely at her house and continued the last two hours to my house alone. The night was dark and cold. I flipped through the radio stations and thought of all that had happened in just a month. It was hard to believe it was all real.

The temperature began dropping quickly as I made my way into and through Tuolumne County with snow falling lightly here and there. With only a few more miles to home, the highway was now thickly covered with snow and empty except for a herd of deer directly in front of me being determinedly led by a large buck. We were met with heavier snowfall as we topped a hill. I flipped the radio off and shook myself out of drowsiness, needing to concentrate more, for driving was becoming more difficult. Putting their heads down, the herd moved into a single-file line up the center of the highway. Being alone in the silence in such heavy snowfall was eerie but peaceful, too, as I inched and fishtailed behind them.

What had happened to my dad, the events and others' outright shocking behaviors in the past month, could have easily been a few chapters read from a horror novel, but it wasn't. It was all real. Now a part of me. Forever a part of my life.

To my ignorance, the utter exhaustion, absurd craziness, responsibilities, and pain had only begun. Not only was the cleanup from the aftermath of the devil's actions just beginning, but so was the strength and brightness of the greatness of our God. For He will be the One who will outshine us all, and it will be His power alone that dominates any rival that enters this arena: "Men shall speak of the might of Your awesome acts, and I will declare Your greatness" (Ps 145:6).

Chapter Seven

So much had happened since that night my God woke me up to pray for my dad. My prayers and that question asked to me by the Almighty set me on a journey that would change my life forever. The course of this journey, though, was completely unknown to me. This was not something I planned for. It was not something I had ever hoped to do.

When I had said "yes" to Dad not many days before his life was cruelly stolen and "yes" to God in my bedroom, I was saying "yes" to this responsibility and all that came with it. What was I supposed to do? How would I know what to do with everything that had to be done, all while being faithful to my earthly and heavenly fathers, representing each in the right light?

This task was beyond my own strength and knowledge. Even so, I stepped forward onto this strange path believing God Himself would be my guide and praying that He would be the supplier of what I needed. But how long would it take? Would I make it to the finish line with my faith and sanity intact? I had no idea. And as time went on, this road would seem to have no end.

This road I traveled was narrow, dark, and bumpy. It had so many unexpected twists and turns. I would anxiously look for the end, as if with one more step I would suffocate and be destroyed, becoming forever lost on this tortuous journey.

On and on I went and all the while with my unwelcomed companion, Murder, in tow. When a life is ended violently at the hands of another, that act has many names, different faces, and feelings that are hard for someone to explain who has lost a loved one in such a way. Often at times I would become impatient, lonely, and afraid—and then desperate—to get off this path and away from my evil travel partner.

I did not get to pick my partner for this journey. I hated walking beside him, I hated everything about him, and I didn't want to be there. I did not open my heart to him. I would not give him my personal attention—the devil would get no glory from me.

Murder is ugly and vile and he's out to destroy lives however he can. Deep within my heart is where I give him names, there only will I face the realities of my suffering and intently look upon who it is that I feel I am forced to walk beside. I call him Thief. He is rage and unimaginable sorrow. Murder is days passing by while the clock stands still. Those evil actions that ended my dad's life are over, but what took place then is not finished and what seemed to be the end was really only the beginning.

Thankfully, Murder was not my only companion. Jesus was also, and as my true guide, He also was not finished, and to Him alone be the glory. But, as you know, fear and frustration can blur our vision. It's His power and mercy that are far greater than anything else in this world, and so only because of Jesus I did not become lost or destroyed. In fact, in many ways I grew stronger along the way. And as I submitted, which put God up front instead of myself, my distorted view became clearer. I learned a lot from my Guide. He also kept me safe, even in those times of terror and through feelings of desperation. God led me on, never wavering, protecting my life and mind, and my family with me.

> I would have lost heart, unless I had believed
> That I would see the goodness of the Lord
> In the land of the living.
> Wait on the Lord;
> Be of good courage,
> And He shall strengthen your heart;
> Wait, I say, on the Lord! (Ps 27:13–14)

This was true here; I would have lost heart and courage if it were not for Jesus. It is only by His power and mercy that I was able to endure for so long and without being destroyed.

My finish line of this long and difficult journey finally comes into sight two-and-a-half years after I was awakened with that undeniable urgency to pray for my dad.

September 3rd, on a Tuesday in a quiet courtroom, is where what has seemed to be an endless mission will now be coming to a close.

At the end of a hall, outside closed courtroom doors, I stand silently, tense and uneasy. Here I am told to wait, for the defendant is late for our 10 a.m. plea time. I have been told Mr. Stewart, the man who brutally murdered, robbed, and committed arson against my dad, was going to plead guilty to all these charges.

Now, as I sit down on a large wooden bench beside the double doors of the courtroom, I am not totally convinced that he is going to plead guilty to the heinous crimes he committed.

DREAMS

I DREAM A LOT. Most of my dreams are really silly and so funny. My family gets annoyed with me at times, as I'm always eager to tell them the latest one. Many involve my mama doing really unusual and hilarious things with all of us with her. She tells me, "Hoppy, you must secretly think I'm crazy." I actually don't, but she's definitely funny, for sure.

Then there have been some dreams that are without a doubt from God, with Him speaking to me on behalf of others to whom I am meant to relay His message.

And there are those that I believe have a purpose and a meaning, but I'm not sure what.

Here to follow is the first of the three dreams that I have had relating to my dad being killed, before this book came to be. The other two come later in the book. These dreams were carefully written down shortly after I had them, expressing just how I saw and experienced them.

First Dream

Dreamt February 2012

I get a call here at home one afternoon from the prosecuting attorney's office telling me that the defendant is finally ready to accept our plea deal, but that it has to be done tomorrow. I am incredibly relieved and tell the attorney that I will be there in the courtroom tomorrow. On such short notice, I do not know how it will be possible to get a flight back to Tennessee and be there on time, but I know I have to—I have to! The attorneys, officers, and myself have been working so hard for this to come, and now it has. I am going.

Now everything comes alive in my dream. Colors, smells, what I hear, feel, think, and touch are all very much real.

I, and strangely enough my husband too, am standing outside the doors of the courtroom where the man who murdered my dad will plead guilty to all of his crimes.

The courtroom is well lit but not at all bright. The air is stale, as though it has been closed up for a long time, and even a bit dusty. Several people are there, filling up the rows of wooden benches in the two columns, which are each directly behind a fine-looking all-oak table desk. These people in the courtroom, all of whom I don't know, are talking with one another and walking slowly between the rows, finding their seats. My husband and I take two seats on the outside of the row in the left column about four rows back from the front.

We are already sitting, but others are not, as they are still talking. I hear a loud voice coming from up front telling us all to take our seats. Now I can easily see attorneys at the two desks who I recognize, along with several officers scattered around, who I also know. In the very front, at a much larger desk than the two near the partition, sits a judge and his team. But I also now see Stephen, my dad's murderer, sitting at the desk with his attorney—the desk in front of the column I am sitting in.

The judge introduces the case and says we are going to get started now. In my hand is the letter I had written to Stephen.

In real life I had written this exact letter to Stephen, but it had already been mailed to him months before. In my dream, though, I still had the letter. It had not been mailed, and I was going to give it to him myself.

With everyone in their seats now and the case introduced, no one is talking. It is quiet except for up front, as the attorneys are talking, discussing the facts amongst each other. I suddenly have an overwhelming feeling that I have to talk to the defendant, give him my letter—right now! When I stand up, I instantly become angry, furious, and so heartbroken all at the same time. These feelings are intense, and I have to do something before I explode from the heat of my anger and sorrow. I storm up the aisle and through the opening between the two areas, not caring what people think or how they may try to stop me. I am going to talk to Stephen, tell him how I feel, what he has done, and tell him how horrible of a person I think he is.

I push through a few officers who try to keep me from reaching the defendant; even the attorneys get in my way, telling me I can't do this—but I don't care what they think or about the rules of the courtroom. There is a commotion, but once I reach Stephen it all stops.

The room is quiet once again. The attorneys, officers, judge, and people in the benched rows are all staring at me. The room is cold now; it smells musky and of sweat and fear. I am even more furious now for having had to push my way up here to do what I feel I must. I didn't really know what I was going to do besides grab hold of this murderer and tell him how much he has hurt me. I want him to be punished for what he did to Dad and to me.

Full of rage and pain, I look down to Stephen as he is sitting, and I am standing over him now. Though, the instant our eyes meet, all of that hatred and fury I had raging within me leaves—all of it. Every bit of nothing less than pure evil that had been about to unleash itself is gone. Now as I look at this murderer sitting in a wheelchair, I feel only pity and sorrow for him. We say nothing; we only look at one another, and my heart now breaks for him. I have not forgotten what he has done, but compassion is now all I feel for him. So, I lean down and put my hand on his forearm as I am overcome by a need to show kindness.

For just an instant when I gently lay my hand on his arm, I can see in his eyes that he sees my heart. There is forgiveness and compassion in me now instead of hatred toward him. But then something flashes in his eyes. The dark but bright flash in his blue eyes is distinct and evil. Whatever is in him now hates what is in me and wants to kill me.

In one swift motion, smooth as glass, this man who is here to plead guilty to murdering my dad pulls a beautiful opal-handled, *wide, steel-bladed knife out from under one of his legs with one hand. He puts the other hand over mine that is still on his arm as I am leaned over. He holds me tight with that hand over mine and, with the other hand, he forcibly drives that beautiful, shiny knife into my chest all the way up to the hilt of the four-inch blade. He pulls, raising himself up in his seat just a little to keep a firm grip on the opal handle of the blade, which has gone fully into my chest at an angle, right above my heart. Luckily, he misgauged his target.*

I cannot believe what he just did. Neither can anyone else. The officers and attorneys rush over to us both. The attorney next to him is up and beside me now, along with my husband.

I only feel an intense burning feeling in my chest around where the knife entered in. Stephen is holding the knife tight into my chest, not loosening his grip on the handle or his force behind it. Hot blood is soaking my dress around the entrance of this stab wound and I can feel it oozing down to my stomach.

The people gathered around are authoritatively telling Stephen to let me go. One officer grabs the defendant and another officer grabs his hand that is holding so tightly to the knife in my chest. My husband is pulling at my arm that Stephen has a hold of while yelling at both of us. Stephen acts as though he doesn't hear anyone or feel their hands on him, either, as they try to pull him away from me.

I also pay no one else any attention. I hear the other people. I know what they are saying, and I can feel them up against me, but I only look at this man who has driven a knife into my chest. I look only at him. I don't speak or resist. I only look into his eyes and feel pity for him. But, his eyes looking back are of cruelty, and then, tilting further up to me, close to my face, he says, quietly but harshly, "I hate you. I hate you." Over and over he says this as people are now aggressively trying to remove his hand from the handle of that knife. The pain in my chest sharpens as the officers begin prying Stephen's fingers one by one from the handle. My heart goes out to him; without ceasing, he has told me how he hates me, but now he is crying as he looks into my eyes. Finally, before Stephen's fingers are all removed from the opal knife handle, he pulls it out by his will and the pulling of the officers. I am free and stagger back. I am weak from the blood loss and my chest is still on fire, but I am alive and standing.

The attorneys tell me that the proceeding must continue but that I need to go to the hospital. I tell them that I am not leaving until the proceeding is over. I tell the attorneys that I have waited, hoped, and prayed for this day and that I have come a long way for this in more ways than just distance. I am staying, I tell them, and then I ask for a towel to hold to the stab wound while the proceeding continues. I am given a towel, and my husband helps me to my seat. Everyone settles down and takes their seats again.

Beside Stephen, lying on the floor is the once beautifully colored, opal-handled knife that is now covered in blood. An officer with a tissue in his hand is there, kneeling down to pick it up off the floor. It is a shame, I think, that something pretty was used to do something ugly.

The proceeding is over and Stephen, the man who murdered my father, pled guilty to all charges. It is over. He had hurt me with his crimes against Dad and with what he did to me today, but God is greater than evil.

Weakened from the blood loss and injuries within, I am assisted out of my seat and into a standing position by a few people who came over to me. One of the court officials makes his way to me, grabbing my arm with a bewildered look on his face. This official, who was in the midst of all that happened up front, looks me dead in the eyes and says, "Did you see what happened?" I answer by telling him, "All I know is what happened between Stephen and I, and what God did in me."

Without any more thought of those people in that courtroom or what happened there, I turn around to leave, because I must now go to the hospital. As I am being helped out of the courthouse, I look down at my dress that is now torn and bloodstained. The sight of it is disturbing, and it makes me feel let down and disheartened.

In my dream I was wearing a new dress, a brand-new dress that I bought, and it was pretty. Most all of my clothes are either hand-me-downs from someone or bought used at a thrift store. So, to have an actual new dress was exciting, even if it was in a dream.

The Final Word

> *My husband and I stand beside an open ambulance that was waiting for me outside the courthouse. I am relieved about what happened between Stephen and I, even though it was strange and scary. I am also very tired, feeling as though I am coming away from myself, but, funnily enough, what I really feel disappointed over is having my new dress ruined.*

About two weeks after having this dream, the kids and I went to the local Walmart to get a few household supplies. As we walked down the main aisle, I looked to my left, and hanging high on a rack was a dress that made me stop. This dress was a distance from me, but I recognized it. As I stood there in the middle of the aisle, staring, I told the kids that I knew that dress. They didn't know what I was looking at. I turned our cart and told Travis, Jacob, and HannahGrace to follow me.

I went straight to the dress and took it off its rack. This was exactly the dress I was wearing in my dream. There were many dresses on this rack, but there was none else like this one. There was just this one and it was my size! Never had I seen this dress before that dream or since, to my knowledge, not on a person or in a store. This dress was expensive for me, and not what I was able to spend money on, but I didn't care what anyone would say or what would happen because I was wasting twenty dollars on myself. I put the dress in my shopping cart without trying it on. It was already mine, it seemed, and held importance worth defending. I bought it.

I still have this dress today and gladly wear it. This dress and I have a story together. My dad's murderer just missed from piercing my heart with his opal-handled knife, but God did not miss. And His blade opened my heart so hatred could be replaced with compassion. I haven't forgotten!

Chapter Eight

"Hurry up and wait" is what I often heard from the attorneys as they described how things moved along in the proceedings of the legal world. This saying has most definitely been true throughout our case.

Issues with Stephen, and his seemingly unmotivated attorney, have held up the legal progression of this case all along, causing me much frustration and disappointments on top of everything else I have been dealing with. Now he is not on time for this very important moment. I have waited so long for this, and I am left waiting and wondering yet again.

Next to me is my mom who came back to Tennessee with me, also hoping to see an end of this case. We whisper to each other, wondering who that couple is sitting across the hall from us. A bailiff opens the double doors before us and says to come in.

My mom and I go inside, with the couple from across the hall following a few paces behind us. After we enter this large, empty courtroom, I turn to the officer and ask him where we are supposed to sit. He tells me we can sit anywhere for now.

The center aisle is wide between two columns with rows of long, padded wooden benches. My mom and I walk to the front bench on the left side and take our seats closest to the center aisle. The couple that followed us in also comes forward, cutting in and walking along the length of the row right behind us. They come around to sit on the same bench as we are on, but at the opposite end. Mom and I both look at the couple on the end and they at us. We each give a friendly smile, but none of us says anything.

Different bailiffs come in and out of a side door, speaking to each other. One then comes to me and says, "It's going to be a while longer before things get going, because the defendant is being transported to court this morning by ambulance, and it has been delayed." Stephen is coming from the special needs prison in Nashville, where he has been held for medical reasons since earlier this year, when he was finally truly arrested (which took two years).

I have waited for this day for so long, not giving up, and now I am told I will have to wait longer. My nerves and strength seem to be coming to a breaking point. I have to keep my composure and strength long enough to cross the finish line. So, I leave the still courtroom to settle myself. I slowly pace and pray alone in the outside hall. It is good to be alone, just God and me, for a few minutes. I feel so twisted inside, afraid, very afraid and nauseous, but also an energy of wantin' a fight. I am going to stand face-to-face with the man who brutally murdered my father, and I know I will not back down from letting my God have His way in this. I have been worried about and a little afraid of what Stephen will look like. Will I recognize him? Will I see in him the evil that has caused us to be here today? I go over to the nearby water fountain and get a drink, take a deep breath, smooth my dress, and go through the double doors again into the courtroom.

I had wanted to wear the dress that I dreamt about and then bought, for it was mine, but because Mama knew of my dream and of all the serious threats that had been made against me throughout this time, she was adamant I not wear it today, in the courtroom. I did want to, though; I was curious whether or not Stephen would show any signs of recognizing it.

It is still very quiet as I go back into that large room, with only the four of us on the front bench. While I had excused myself, the young woman who sat opposite of us told my mom that I must not remember who she is. When I sit down, the young woman turns toward my mom and me, telling me how she was just saying that I must not remember her. She reminds us her name is Laura (though I know her best by her nickname, Pooh).

Chapter Eight

So far this morning I have only seen this woman from the side and at a distance. She has seemed familiar, but my mind has been so preoccupied that I haven't given her familiarity much thought. Now that she is facing me and I am paying attention, I know who she is: one of Stephen's younger sisters. She looks very much like her mom, very pretty. I am glad to see her and, smiling, I tell her that—but I wish we were somewhere else, not in a courtroom and not about to face what we are going to. It would have been nice to catch up with her. I have some nice memories of being with her mom and all those kids of hers. I like them, a few of them a lot, even though we are not close.

I now learn that the man sitting next to Stephen's sister is her husband and that they live in Alabama. She then continues to tell me that she only knew her brother was going to be in court today because she saw it posted. I ask her how all the other kids have been doing.

For some time throughout the investigations, I had talked to Stephen's dad, and he would tell me of all the troubles brewing in the family over what had happened—not so much with what had happened to my dad; it was Stephen they have been most concerned with. Many never seemed to consider how I must have felt. I was closest to my dad, but my feelings, my grief, did not seem to matter to many.

Laura begins telling me how the turmoil between all the kids—with each turning against the other over Stephen—has gotten bad, to the point that now there is hardly anyone speaking to one another. I respond saying how sad that is to hear, because I know how close they all had been once. But if my Granny Mae were still alive, there's no doubt the trouble these people have been having would be miniscule compared to what she'd unleash on the whole mess of 'em. The hell they'd all pay would be unlike anything they've ever seen for murdering her son. Dad loved his mama dearly, and she did him also; he was most definitely his mother's son. She had passed away thirteen years before my dad's death. His father had died many years before then, and his younger brother just a couple of years earlier than Dad. Not any of them even made it to 60 years old.

My mom tells our relatives who sit at the far end of the bench how it has been a sad time all the way around for everyone, and that she is sorry. My mom asks her if she has seen Stephen, and she says, "No, not since visiting him at the hospital in Knoxville."

After committing the inexcusable, violent crimes against Dad, Stephen tried to kill himself not far from Interstate 40, as he was heading back to east Tennessee. But he was unsuccessful, receiving only major injuries instead, and was taken to a trauma hospital in Knoxville. The account of the accident and the injuries Stephen received was told to me by an officer early on, from the first rough reports. As explained, those critical injuries came about through a dramatic chain of events that showed how determined this man was to end his life. In the first attempt he drove off the roadway and into a tree that was near a bridge that went across the highway. Since that had not done the job, Stephen next climbed up to the top of that cold, lifeless bridge to hang himself with the belt he was wearing. He then cinched the belt around his neck and hooked it onto a piece of rebar sticking out from the bridge. This strap, which Stephen thought would be his ticket out, then broke from the weight of his desperate lunge, causing him to fall to the unmerciful water and earth below. So, instead of what he hoped would be an immediate escape from the reality of the crimes he committed and the consequences that were due, Stephen's efforts only resulted in irreversible damage to his body.

My cousin should have died. He deserved to die for so cruelly killing my dad, making him suffer without a cause, but God did not want Stephen's life to end just yet. So God used a Tennessee State Trooper who quickly found Stephen, and a deputy who kept him from drowning by holding his head up out of the water of the small creek he fell into. Because my dad's wallet with all of his identification and money in it was found in the car Stephen was driving (the car he had stolen before he went to my dad's house),

Chapter Eight

the officers knew this man was involved in something far worse than just a highway accident.

So it was in a hospital room at the bedside of this thirty-eight-year-old murder suspect that the investigator for the Coffee County D.A., along with other officers, began the questioning.

Chapter Nine

It has been only the four of us in this courtroom after being brought in, but bailiffs are now coming in and out again, along with the defense attorney, Mr. Askren, who comes in from the front left side door. He looks at all of us on the front row, gives me a slight courteous nod, and then goes to the far end of the bench where Stephen's sister and her husband are sitting, saying hello to them both.

I had met Mr. Askren a little over a week ago in the district attorney's office. I had flown to Tennessee alone to look through evidence with the wonderful prosecuting Assistant District Attorney Kristy West, who I was so grateful to have leading the way in representing my dad and the laws of the state. She and I, as well as others in the D.A.'s office who I had gotten to know during this two-and-a-half-year journey, were preparing for a trial we all thought would have to happen but never wanted. From both the prosecuting and victim's standpoints, the defendant accepting a plea deal is far better than going to trial. This is hoped for even more so in an area like ours. Here, too often a jury has let a defendant walk even when the evidence clearly proves that person committed the crime. "Not guilty" is a way to "stick it to the man" for those who are against the law and the people who enforce it.

That trip over a week ago was very productive, but also dreadfully difficult for me, as I had to look through pictures of the crime scene along with a few articles of physical evidence.

Chapter Nine

When the large cardboard box was brought into the office and the officer cut it open, I was surprised to see ash on top of the many taped-shut paper bags that filled the box. It even still had a faint smell of a fire to it. I held in my hands different pieces of clothing and personal articles, identifying what were my dad's and which would be Stephen's. How strange it was, holding these things, feeling them, knowing where they had been and what they were a part of.

I answered the questions I was asked by Ms. West and the officer in the room, but I did not feel as though I was there seeing the things I was. I didn't want to be there. After over two years now of reading and listening to dozens of reports and briefings, seeing the evidence of the brutality of the crime, I understood what my dad went through. There were findings that brought the murderer's frighteningly calloused mindset in that moment to light and discoveries I dare not bring myself to speak of or even write. The evidence is a witness to how hard Dad fought and suffered as his life was being violently taken away by the man whose pants I was now holding up.

I was silent and sick to my stomach until late that night. After leaving the D.A.'s office, I remember mindlessly stopping at a nearby restaurant for some strange reason on my way back to the motel I was staying in. Once inside, I sat myself at a table in the corner, seeking a place to hide from the world. I didn't want to be alone either and was too afraid to go back to my room. At this moment what I wanted more than anything was for all this and my life to end. I just sat there not looking at anyone and not saying a word, not even to the waitress when she tried to talk to me. Finally, after only getting complete silence and tears from me, she brought me a piece of pie and a glass of water, saying only, "Honey, it will be alright." She never came back to my table not even with a bill. I tore a napkin in half, wrapping my pie in it and writing "Thank You" on the other half, and left.

All week I was calm and composed, taking care of what I had to with whom I had to, but when I was alone and in the stillness of my motel room, I was deeply troubled, drained, and so crushed within my heart and spirit. I would have been lost—broken—if not for my God.

Only a couple days after I returned home from preparing for a trial, Ms. West called me to let me know that things were suddenly happening very quickly from the defendant's side after my brief meeting with Mr. Askren. The most recent plea deal we had offered was now accepted. I had been determined in my prayers for some time that the right plea deal would be accepted so there would be no trial. God had answered my prayers in my favor. He had not left or turned His back on me during this despised journey.

After greeting his client's sister, Mr. Askren asks her if Stephen's father is going to be here today. He tells her how he had called to let him know about the court date. Laura tells Mr. Askren that he is not coming. She is the only one to be here on behalf of her brother today. The attorney then tells her that it is still going to be a while because Stephen has not arrived.

Ms. West then comes in through the same side door others have been busily coming in and out of all morning. She comes over to me smiling, hugs me, and introduces herself to my mom, and I introduce my mom to her. Ms. West looks at me and says, "It's going to happen today. Are you ready?"

"Yes, I've waited a long time for this," I reply.

She then tells my mom and me that there have been many holdups with the defendant this morning, but he is on his way now. "Good," we respond with relief. Ms. West explains to us now that, because of the holdups, we should leave and come back at 12:15 p.m., for everything should be set to go by 12:30 p.m. My cousin is also listening to what is being said, and we all know we are not being asked but told to leave the courthouse for now.

To be told to leave after I have come so far is a blow I did not expect, and it takes my breath away. I stand mute and expressionless, only giving a nod that I understand.

I don't want to leave, and none of the others seems willing to go, either; but staying in this room that I have fought so hard to get to is not an option, for one of the bailiffs is holding the double doors open, authoritatively motioning for us to exit.

I am even more nervous now and worried, too, that maybe this day that I have so exhaustively prayed and worked for, stretching myself almost to the breaking point, may now not happen. I am sorely distressed thinking that, if I leave the courtroom at this time, what is supposed to happen will all end, unfinished, leaving my hopes completely destroyed. Because here is where I feel the finish line to this remarkable journey I have been on has been marked out, and I must cross it. If not, then what has happened between my dad, God, and myself will all seem in vain.

All together we walk out of that courtroom and down different hallways, but before we go out of the courthouse doors, one of the two elderly security officers stops my mom and me. Then, for some unknown reason, he begins telling us about all the places he has been.

The security officer happily tells of his travels. He is friendly and the stories are interesting, but neither one of us is able to give him the attention he seeks. After politely letting the security officer know we need to leave, we step out and drive back to the hotel we were staying at in town.

Back at our room, my mom decides that she might as well drink one of the smoothies she has while we wait. Mom and I are usually very lighthearted and silly with one another; now we are strangely quiet. I just sit on the edge of the bed watching the clock. With each tick of the secondhand I grow equally more excited, angry, and nervous. The end is drawing nigh, and the devil best get outta my way.

Chapter Ten

I HAVE BEEN ANXIOUSLY waiting for this day, praying for this day, even gut-wrenchingly fearing this day. Do you understand? No! It has felt like no one understands. Don't you see that the importance of this day has consumed me? And not just this long-hoped-for day in court, but the entirety of all that has happened, along with the many roles and responsibilities that I've carried. Truly, even I have not fully understood it all.

The weight of this case, the magnitude of this story, has lain heavily on my shoulders. The responsibility for truth and justice, the mending of broken lives, and the need for integrity have been handed solely to me by everyone involved. My thoughts, my heart, my energy, and my life have been overrun by murder, business, and increased difficulties in my own home. All these things and more were piled on me higher and higher with the weight going unchecked.

Often, by many of those I dealt with, I have been treated as though I am just some random hired (unpaid) person to take care of all of this. They have acted like and spoken to me as though I have no personal feelings in this matter, or if I do, they obviously aren't important—even though the relationship my dad and I shared was closer than any he had with others. By some I was seen for who I am, and to a point my feelings were somewhat considered, but a line was drawn and the responsibilities of it all were still laid upon me. Then there was the one I needed most, my husband, who just stepped back and left me standing fearfully alone in the dark like he always had during other difficult times in our life.

Chapter Ten

As mentioned before, even some of the close family members of the murderer contacted me, expecting me to help them, all while blaming me for Stephen's troubles. So many ugly, cruel, and vulgar things were said to me to my face or over the phone in both California and Tennessee. There were also numerous threats made against my safety, my body, and the progress being made in the case. Some of the threats or incidences from the heartless people I was being tormented by were very scary to me.

More and more through each situation I would see how my true Defender was God. When an officer came to me with news of the outcome from one of those vexing times, the reality of Him fighting our battles was proven to me. As that officer was sharing the fate of one who had come against me, I instantly yet clearly heard my God, as though whispering in my ear, say to me, "Touch not my anointed, and do my prophets no harm" (in reference to the passage in 1 Chr 16:22). This man was found dead shortly after he and his fellow troublemaker had been following me in their car. They had been physically blocking my ways with their car, persistently harassing me and threatening me with violence during one of the times I was in Tennessee to take care of matters for my dad. Like in other instances that had happened throughout this journey, I knew God had taken care of the situation Himself. His purpose and how He was using me was not going to be hindered.

This whole business involved far more than just the evil acts of murder. It was complex, deep, and the tentacles of my responsibilities, burdens, duty, and heartache spread out wide in all directions. No matter my needs or feelings, no matter what was going on within me or around me, I knew that I still had a job to do; I promised Dad I would.

With the strength and guidance God has been mercifully giving me, I have been determined to get this job done, to see it through to the very end no matter how long it takes. *But please, God, let this day be the finish line we've all worked so hard for!*

The bell for round two is ringing. It is now time to go back to the courthouse to take our places once again. My God, I believe, will now take center stage in what I hope will be the final leg of our journey. I stand up from the bed I have been sitting on while listening to my mom try to bring light into our situation, as she always does, and I go into our bathroom to pray one last time. I pray to my Heavenly Father that He would be with me. I ask for Him to speak through me and that it would be Him alone who would be seen as being in control of the courtroom and this situation—that it would be clear He has been all along.

I also pray about the copy of the letter I had written to Stephen, which I had brought with me. When I had written it, I mailed it to the D.A.'s office in order for it to be given to him by his defense attorney, but I don't know if my letter was ever given to the defendant. So, I'm bringing the copy with me in case he had not received it. I finish praying and check myself in the mirror, looking to see if I am really ready. Yes, I am nervous, but I know I am ready.

When I come out of the bathroom, I can tell Mama is nervous, too, but not afraid. She also is ready to face whatever may come our way today.

It was my mom—Mama or Mommy is all I call her because of our close bond—it was her right from the start all the way up until today who has been on my side. Throughout it all she would pray with me, for me, encourage me, make me laugh, be someone I could count on and trust. Yes, it was me who was spoken to in that midnight hour two-and-a-half years ago and called upon to pick up and carry this exhaustive nightmare for so long, but without fail she has been cheering me on, listening, and helping where she can.

Also, Travis, Jacob, and Hannah were kind and patient with me in their own ways during this time, even in the midst of their own grief and anger from missing their Papa. I am so grateful God has allowed me to have them, raise and love them. May they all know how treasured they are and always will be.

Mom and I both know that in the courtroom today things might get ugly. What is expected can easily become something unexpected. Minds, proceedings, outcomes might all change very quickly as we resume our places today.

Chapter Ten

The truth of God and His power is unchangeable, and undoubtedly I know His will will prevail in all of this. But it is *how* God wants all of this, this horrific chapter in my life, to play out and come to a close that I do not know.

So many lives have been involved, each with its own legitimate, valued feelings and parts in this lengthy story, but the leading characters have been God, my dad, the murderer, and myself. Together, we alone were there when the curtains opened, the trailhead gate unlocked, and we together will be crossing the finish line. Connected as we were in the beginning of all this, so shall we be now at the end, with God in His rightful seat ruling as the Judge that He is.

Chapter Eleven

THE MOMENT HAS COME and the stage for the final act is set. Directly behind prosecuting Assistant D.A. Kirsty West and her hard-working aid, my mom and I sit where we are told to, on the right side of the courtroom in the front row. Far behind us is a newspaper reporter and a few officials. Up front to the left of the center aisle is my cousin and her husband directly behind the desk of the defendant's attorney, Mr. Askren. Before us all, hugging the wall on a respected, raised platform, is a clean, rich, long, continuous wooden bench flowing in a gentle semicircle.

The necessary people in what I believe will be the last mile marker to this seemingly never-ending journey have all taken their places: the court reporters, aids, attorneys, different officers and bailiffs. We are all here except for the judge and the defendant. Most importantly, though, God is here.

I can feel the anticipation, the nervousness, and even the authority rising in this large, quiet room. Yet, through the unknown and my uneasiness, I can definitely feel our God rising up in me more and more with each passing heartbeat.

I was told that the defendant had requested permission to speak to the court and myself. I was also asked if I would like to have time to speak during this proceeding, and I had said yes.

Making it known that I would like to address a murderer directly has made me worry about what I should say. I want to say what I feel I need to for my own sake, but I also want to make sure I allow, no, not hinder, what God is wanting to say or do.

Chapter Eleven

Because I have a quiet, shy personality and don't like to be out front, knowing I am going to speak to the officials of the courtroom and to the one who murdered my dad, even though I know him, has made me nervous. *God is greater than any fears or weaknesses in me, and He will have His way here today, in all of us.* I have to remind myself of this.

Suddenly, a door opens for the first time on my right, which we all turn our attention to. Out come a couple of deputies followed by a raised gurney that is being pushed by another deputy. On that gurney, which has the top half adjusted to an upright position, sits the man who confessed to killing my beloved father and friend, my children's cherished Papa, a man who was respected and loved by many. The defendant is being wheeled in on a gurney instead of walking in because he is paralyzed from the waist down along with having one leg partially amputated as a result from his self-inflicted wounds after killing my dad.

My disgraceful cousin is positioned beside his attorney, facing the bench. Stephen only looked forward as he was brought into the courtroom and still looks forward now, beside Mr. Askren, never turning toward me or anyone else. The extra deputies go out the same door they had just come through. The door is shut, and we all seem to take a breath, for it's fixin' to start.

A bailiff steps forward and with a loud, in-charge kind of voice tells everyone to stand as the honorable Judge Jackson comes out of her chambers and into the courtroom. After the judge takes her appointed seat, we then are told we can also take our seats.

The case was originally given to a judge who was known for his strength and conservative values, which the prosecuting team and myself appreciated. But, as time passed through this long journey, our case was, to my disappointment at the time, turned over to the judge who was known for having certain liberal views I'd hoped not to have in the one presiding over something as important as this.

I have seen this judge in action, though. It was during a past hearing where case after shocking case was brought before her, including this one—and she was not pleased at all with how long it had been delayed. The judge made it clear she wanted this case to come to a close. She was not the only one. After seeing how this judge conducted herself and the professionalism she displayed that day during the hearings, I was no longer concerned that it was she who'd be ruling over our case.

Circuit Court Judge Jackson introduces the case of the State of Tennessee v. Stephen Floyd Stewart to the nearly empty courtroom. The prosecutor, Assistant D.A. Kirsty West, stands up, addressing the judge as she clearly paints a picture with her words of the disgusting events involved in the inexcusable crimes committed against my dad.

One by one the charges are brought forth as agreed upon in the hard-fought-for plea deal. The Honorable Judge Jackson looks the defendant, Stephen Stewart, in the eyes and asks with a clear, stern, yet still feminine voice, "What does Mr. Stewart plead to each specific charge against him?" Without hesitation and with a steady voice the defendant answers the judge with, "Guilty, your Honor"—to second-degree murder, attempted aggravated arson, aggravated robbery, and theft over $1,000. These crimes together totaled to a maximum of thirty-five years as punishment in prison.

Thank you, Lord. I have waited so long to hear those words, "Guilty, your Honor," from the defendant. He has stalled, played the victim, and caused so many unnecessary hardships in this case, but no more. He has willingly and publicly pled guilty to the crimes he committed—with lesser degrees as part of his deal.

Judge Jackson asks Stephen if he has anything he would like to say. He states, "Yes." Earlier that morning Ms. West told me that she felt I needed to be aware Mr. Stewart has for some time now been spewing out hatred and poison for me. She protectively asked me to prepare myself for his foul language and the bitterness he has toward me that was sure to come out.

I am standing to his right now, just a couple of feet behind Ms. West, but I move forward so as to be facing more in Stephen's direction. This man who just pled guilty to killing my dad suddenly

Chapter Eleven

turns his head and shifts his body to his right in order to face me. We lock eyes almost immediately, and with focused intent he sees me now for the first time here and, really, I him. Even with the fact that I've known him I feel no sense of familiarity looking at Stephen now. With our eyes fixed on one another, it seems as though it is only the two of us in this room. I had wondered if I would recognize my cousin when this day came, and here, now, at this moment, I don't. My heart feels as though it is going to explode from pounding so hard. *I am afraid.*

> The LORD is my light and my salvation; whom shall I fear? The LORD is the strength of my life; of whom shall I be afraid? When the wicked came against me to eat up my flesh, my enemies and foes, they stumbled and fell. Though an army may encamp against me, my heart shall not fear; though war may rise against me, in this I will be confident. (Ps 27:1–3)

I take a deep breath and set my stance. This isn't over. This all-consuming journey isn't finished yet. I must face what has to be done here so my God's will shall be done regarding my purpose in all this.

Still looking at me, Stephen begins to cry. I become angry at the sight of his tears. I am not quick-tempered, but seeing this murderer cry as he is propped up on his gurney while looking at me sickens me—it infuriates me!

I stand silent, intensely staring into his eyes as my anger builds within me. Stephen does not turn away. He clears his throat and begins.

"I want you to know I am sorry," this man who stole my dad from me says. He continues, saying that he doesn't know what came over him. He says that we are family and that he loves us all. Stephen tells me that he hopes I can forgive him, but if I can't, that would be okay. "I wish I could change places with Junior. Your dad didn't deserve what happened to him," he tells me.

This distant cousin of mine begins talking about his close family members and, also, our very large extended family, and how it is all torn apart because of him, and how he is now hated for it. Still crying, Stephen says he hopes my brother, along with two of our close cousins, aren't with those who hate him and that someday, he hopes, they will be able to forgive him.

Even though my eyes have never left his as he has been speaking, nor has my stance before him weakened, yet I now begin to see this man more clearly, and with this clarity, the heat and fierceness of my anger subsides. I can now see he is a person also and not just a murderer, something that I had lost sight of along the way.

Again, Stephen tells me that he is sorry for what he has done. He says to me that his life doesn't mean anything now, and that he is going to hell, so he wants to die and get it over with. Stephen looks down and says no more.

Chapter Twelve

THIS MAN BEFORE ME whom I have stood here listening to is the one who brutally ended my dad's life. He caused me so much pain, which has forever changed my life and the lives of many others, also. He came here today prepared to speak to me. He even wrote down what he wanted to say and started his speech with the guidance of his notes, but he soon put them down to speak on his own. Yes, Stephen is sorry, I know that he is, but I can see from looking at him, I can feel from the tones of his voice, that the entirety of his repentance is not for the crimes and sins he has committed. He seems to be more sorrowful for the state his body is in and the years in prison he was just sentenced to as punishment.

I am now told by Ms. West that it is my turn to speak. My mama is close, standing just slightly behind me, but I am afraid, dreadfully afraid, of what I should say, of what God wants me to say. My heart pounds within me as I silently pray. God is going to have His say here today. Something is going to happen, that I am sure of. Jesus has had a hand in this whole ordeal from the start, and He will be ending it here today. How He so graciously allowed me to be a part of it all, even now, I will forever be in awe of.

I am grateful, truly, as difficult and heart-wrenching as it is, I am thankful for this moment. As I open my mouth and begin to speak, all fear and nervousness leaves me, and my heart steadies. Our God really is greater than all things, especially my fears.

> "Therefore prepare yourself and arise, and speak to them all that I command you. Do not be dismayed before their faces, lest I dismay you before them. For behold, I have

made you this day a fortified city and an iron pillar, and bronze walls against the whole land—against the kings of Judah, against its princes, against its priests, and against the people of the land. They will fight against you, but they shall not prevail against you. For I am with you," says the LORD, "to deliver you." (Jer 1:17–19)

My greatest purpose here today is to say and do what my God has intended for me, but I also told God that I, too, need to say what I must on my own behalf.

I begin telling Stephen right from the start of the realities of what he did to my dad. I say, "Stephen, my dad, yes Stephen, *my* dad, had helped you, others in your family, people all around him, and you then chopped him to death, stole his hard-earned money, and tried to burn him to cover it up. No one deserves to die like that!" I emphasize "my dad" because of a statement Stephen had made saying Junior was also his dad early on in the investigation. An officer had asked me to find the truth of this claim, which turned out to be false. Amazingly, I am calm; and, only by the grace of God, I have compassion now for this man before me. I speak loud enough for Stephen to hear me, but throughout it all I never raise my voice. I continue telling him that he is right, he has caused a huge mess, tearing our families apart, and that he has hurt a lot of people. I tell Stephen how I have tried to protect his dad, how I stood up for him, and that I even had his dad be one of the pallbearers helping to carry my dad's casket to his final resting place buried close to his brother and their parents at our family's graveyard. Stephen thanks me.

I say, "You made my dad suffer. What you did was disgusting, and without any reason you hurt him and me. I loved my dad and was closer to him than anyone else, and you killed him, took him from me."

Now I actually feel God step forward within me, and my time is done.

"Stephen, what you did wasn't right in any way, and not only did you hurt us, you sinned against God. But still, you are not beyond His forgiveness or His love. You were not created to be a

Chapter Twelve

murderer. God Almighty created you Himself for good and not evil. The horrible things you did to my dad, how you have hurt our family and even yourself is deserving of hell, but it doesn't have to be." I tell Stephen how I have done a lot of things in my life that I am not proud of, how I have sinned also and am in need of God's forgiveness. "If I do not forgive you, Stephen, then I will not be forgiven. I forgive you."

My attention has been on Stephen this whole time, only looking directly at him. After I say I forgive him, something to my right catches the corner of my eye. I turn my head in that direction and I see a tissue box being passed from person to person up front along the bench. Tears and emotions are flowing from the judge, court reporter, and other officials of this courtroom. There is a sense of awe from the strong presence of our Savior that is undeniable in this room, and I am about to see why.

As I turn my head and attention back to Stephen, I see, several feet above him, a large softly colored form spread out but held together. This beautiful sight is not dense or solid, but it is of substance. Within seconds of seeing this wonder, I believe I know what it is. What is hovering over Stephen is the power of God; it is forgiveness. This, what I am clearly seeing, what I can undeniably feel, what my spirit is being drawn to and excited about is absolutely forgiveness that could have only come from the Lord Jesus Christ.

The Spirit of God is here, bearing witness to the fact that He and the surety of His forgiveness are alive and real. I don't know if anyone else in the courtroom sees this cloud-like form as it takes on almost iridescent, but not shiny, hues of pinks, greens, and blues. The looks I saw a moment ago on people's faces make me think they saw something, but if not, I do believe they know that the presence of the one and only true living God is with us.

I prayed that God would have His way here today, and He is. Of course, Jesus will have His way whether I ask for it or not. He is all-powerful, all-knowing, beautiful, and glorious.

As I stand here looking back at Stephen, this murderer, this poor soul our Savior is willing and ready to forgive so graciously,

I myself am overwhelmed by His power and mercy pouring into me.

    Even though I had told this vicious killer before me that I forgave him (and I really thought I had meant it), I now can truly feel it. I have prayed throughout this entire journey for forgiveness to come. I unbegrudgingly said I forgave him and even expressed my forgiveness in a letter to him. I wanted to believe my heart and words were true. But, by a mighty act of God, I found out that even though I said "I forgive" and felt it, hoped for it, my forgiveness was only on the surface and my heart wasn't pure. God is showing Himself here, and as His Holy Spirit floods my entire being, I can feel Stephen being released from me, along with all the anger and bitterness I had stitched into my heartache and fears. A whole new understanding of what forgiveness is and what it feels like, along with the importance of it, has opened up, been revealed to me. It isn't just Stephen I am being set free from and forgiving. I instantly forgive all, completely, inside and out; there is nothing hidden or unreached. I forgive in a way I never thought possible. I am being healed of the wounds from all who have hurt or wronged me throughout my life and of the sinful feelings I myself have harbored against them. I too am forgiven. It is God alone doing this within me; it is not by my efforts. So mercifully my God is ministering to me, to all who are willing to hear Him, right here in this moment. I came today wanting whoever would be here to know that our Savior, our God, is real and that He does care about them. I believe it's being proven. The devil will not triumph over all that has happened during the past two-and-a-half years.

My dad's life ended in a way no one's should. He is gone, and I very much miss him, and forever on this earth I will. But my God is healing me, setting me free. I never once thought or even imagined that Jesus would see my heart, my fears, loneliness, and struggles here in this courtroom or all along. I only thought He would see and minister to, make Himself known to, the defendant and those present with us.

Chapter Twelve

    I knew God was going to make Himself known today. I knew that His will would be done on His own and by using me, but I had not considered that Jesus would do something in me, for me, besides calming and guiding me for His purpose. Yet, right here in front of everyone, He pierces my heart, cutting me open so all the poison can flow out. God sees it all as He washes me clean.

    I, like most of us, have read about forgiveness, talked about it, and purposely said that I forgive. We try our best to walk that out in our lives and within relationships, but through what I just amazingly encountered, I've learned it's so much more than that. Forgiveness, forgiveness that can only come from God, is real; it is powerful and incredibly beautiful. Here before me, before all of us in this room, forgiveness is alive. It has taken form, and its importance, its power and purpose, is undeniable. What I am literally seeing before me and feeling is far more than anything I have read or heard about forgiveness before.

Chapter Thirteen

TRULY JESUS IS THE Savior of us all. Even if no one in this entire world believed in Him or accepted Him for who He is, it would not in any way diminish His power, His sovereignty, or the truth of creation's past or future. I remember it being said in a teaching once that who and what God is was shown in the life, death, and resurrection of Jesus. Yes, it was the Word of God who brought the universe into life and, still, it is the Word, the Spirit of God, who saves us now, if only we would accept.

I perceive this; the light and power of forgiveness that I see in the courtroom may not be believed or understood, either. But I know what I feel, what I have been hearing God say, and the miraculous healing that's taking place within me from Him alone.

I wonder what God is doing in the hearts of these people in the courtroom. I know I will always remember this day. Would they?

Years later my dear mama was asked what she remembers of that incredible event which she had been a vital part of. She allowed her heart and mind to travel back, pulling forward the box of memories and emotions she had carefully packed away. Unfolding the pieces she took from the courtroom, she saw it all again. Closing her eyes to see the piece she was holding more clearly, Mom began to recall how what she felt like had been a feeling of tension in the room was replaced with a presence of power emanating from within me. She continued, saying that everyone seemed to feel it as they watched me, and that it truly felt like there was this other presence in the room.

Chapter Thirteen

Forgiveness being revealed in such a dramatic way today is not the only thing that happens. I continue speaking without any hesitations or nervousness for a bit more. I say we all deserve to go to hell no matter how "good" we might think we are, but because of Jesus, we have a way to be washed clean, forgiven, and set free from hell. Words pour into me and I freely speak, but honestly, I do not know all that I say, for it is God who is having His say, and it isn't about me.

The room is quiet. It has been all the while I've been speaking. People are listening. Oh, I hope they know who has actually been speaking here this day and His heart in all this. May God give us all understanding.

When I and God are done and the legal matters are settled, the attorneys and court officials begin gathering up their things. The Honorable Judge Jackson dismisses the court and then a deputy opens her chamber's door for her, but she passes him by and instead comes down out onto the courtroom floor to me. The judge extends her arm, taking my hand that I extend to her, but she doesn't shake my hand, she only holds it. While holding my outstretched hand, Judge Jackson tells me that it took a lot of courage for me to do what I did. She says that she had never before seen anything like what took place in her courtroom today, and that it is hard to believe. I continue to hold her hand and only say, "Thank you, ma'am, it was God here today, it was God." What else could I say? With a smile and a nod Judge Jackson lets go of my hand, turns, and quickly makes her way into her chambers.

Standing near me is Assistant D.A. West, who now looks at me with a funny, wide-eyed expression and says, "Wow, that's not like her to have done that." Ms. West comes in close to my mom and me now and tells us how perfect it all has turned out. She tells me that she is proud of how well I handled myself. Ms. West asks if I am happy with how this case turned out, if I had said all I wanted to. I tell her that I am happy with the plea deal we had agreed on. I am glad the defendant was able to speak to me, and I thank her for allowing me to say all I needed to today and all along. I wonder if Dad would've been pleased with what's been happening in here?

Our district attorney's office, the numerous detectives, investigators, and various other attorneys and officers worked so hard right from the beginning and throughout this long, difficult—very difficult—two-and-a-half-year journey. I hug Ms. West and repeatedly thank her, telling her how I appreciate her and her whole team, how kind they all were to me. My precious, supportive mama stood by my side during this whole proceeding and now she, too, hugs Ms. West and thanks her. My mother then comes to me with that beautiful smile of hers and hugs me also.

During this time of talking, Stephen is taken back through the door he had come in by earlier to where he will await being loaded back into the ambulance and taken to prison. An officer comes up to me telling me that Mr. Stewart would like to talk to me there in the room he's being held in. The deputy says to me quietly that I do not have to go in there and talk to Mr. Stewart if I do not want to. I tell the officer that it's okay, I will let him talk to me. I don't know what he wants to say or how his attitude would be now, and so I am a little worried. Plus, I do not know how close, physically, I would have to be to him. This time here, what God wants to do, all that has needed to be done, what is meant to be done, has to be finished and completed, and so I'll go.

I give a smile to the officer to show I am ready, then turn with a smile also to Ms. West and my mom. I take a deep breath then ask Ms. West if there is anything else I have to do? She says there is and asks for me to come to the district attorney's office tomorrow to take care of all I need to. I tell her okay, and that I will see her later, thanking her again.

Still in my hand is the letter I had brought here into this courtroom to either give or read to Stephen, in case he had never gotten it originally when I sent it to him. I now put it away in my little purse.

I did not tell you that, early on, when it was my time to speak during the proceeding, while I was only speaking for myself, I asked

Chapter Thirteen

Stephen if he ever received the letter I had written to him and if he had read it. Stephen said that he had gotten it and that he had read it. Then, with a tone and expression I had heard and seen of him in that dream I had had over a year ago, he says, "Jenny, I don't hate you." Just like in my dream, but its opposite. How strange it is that my feelings and some of the things that have happened here in real life so strongly reflect how they were in the dream that I had forgotten.

I follow the deputy forward and to the right of where I have been standing as he holds the door open for me into the room where Mr. Stewart is being held, with my mom right behind me.

The barren room is small with only a couple of chairs along the wall. There is a door open opposite the door we come in through, and this door is a passageway to the outside, where I see an ambulance close by, parallel with the wall. But I also see sunshine, freedom, fresh air, and I want to run out of here, leaving all this behind in a mad-dash escape.

Is Stephen thinking the same thing I am as he looks out? That short distance between the courthouse and ambulance will be the last physical feeling of freedom he will have on this earth. Will Stephen know this, as he crosses over that threshold into the light, breathing in the humid air of this sense of home he knows so well?

How terribly desperate and alone a prisoner must surely feel is sad, but crimes do not have to be committed. This is not Stephen Stewart's first time breaking the law. He has been guilty of other crimes, even one similar to this now, though not as drastic or brutal as what he did to Dad. It is a shame he did not learn from his mistakes.

He had been incarcerated for his previous crimes, but he did not serve much time for them. Obviously, it was not long enough to deter him from continuing down the path of violence. I'm sure Stephen was probably starting to think he wouldn't do any real time for killing my dad either, since it was two years before he was actually arrested. Charges were brought against him while he was still in the hospital recovering from his attempted suicide, but from there he was only placed on a type of house arrest. He lived in an actual home with one of his brothers in East Tennessee, still able to enjoy being with family and the pleasures of life, which bothered me immensely. I felt it wasn't right and painfully unfair. I was not able to be with my dad and enjoy our family being together with him because Stephen, in a horrifying way, ended Dad's life.

He did not learn from his mistakes before, and now today he has lost everything of this world. The only home he'll know from now on is the prison. But God showed up today and is giving Stephen the chance to leave this place with something far greater than everything he's lost of this world—Himself.

Chapter Fourteen

IN THE CENTER OF that small, uninviting holding room is a violent, now properly convicted felon who has asked to speak with me one last time. On one side of his gurney a few steps back is the defense attorney and his aid. On the opposite side is my mama and me, and a few steps even further back, and near the door to the outside, is a deputy keeping a close watch on us all.

As I said, the room was small with not many options for where to stand, especially given how the gurney was positioned. I do not like being this close to him, seeing him so clearly. I am very uncomfortable being in this room, so near an actual murderer, this relative I once knew, and my uneasiness must show on my face, because the deputy near the door gives me a kind smile. The defense attorney speaks up, saying that he thanks me for being willing to come in here, since his client had asked to speak to me alone and this was as alone as it could be.

I look at Stephen and tell him how thankful I am that he finally was willing to accept a plea deal and save us all from a court trial. "Thank you for making this possible here today and bringing it all to a close," I say.

Stephen looks up at me, and now with true sincerity in his voice, he asks if all I said was true? I tell him that it was and that it was from God. I say, "Did you hear what was said, Stephen, that still with all that you have done you are not beyond God's forgiveness or love?"

My dear ones, do you hear that? Sin is sin, one not greater than the other. All sin is hurtful, ugly, destructive, and against our

Creator's will, but we can be forgiven. This man before me now, looking and speaking to me, committed horrifying acts of violence. But Jesus told him that still he was not beyond His forgiveness or love. I think that's incredible.

It is hard for me to fully understand. I myself struggle with not knowing if my Lord actually sees me or even knows me. Does He really love me for who I am individually and not just as one piece rolled into the clay ball of humanity? That may sound strange, but it is something I honestly wonder about. I want to be used by God, truly I do, and I am so very grateful for the times He has used me. I am thankful for the many words and dreams He has given me. I am not certain, though, if the incredible mercy, kindness, and strength God has shown to me and given to me so many times are gifts generously handed to a mere servant with no real worth, or could He, does He, see me as something more? Someone worth knowing, someone worth being loved? I don't know if I am. Enough of my own self; there is more to this story.

After I remind Stephen of what God has said to him, he asks me if I believe it. I tell him that it was Jesus who told him that he was not beyond His forgiveness or love. Everything said out there was to him, for him, and I believe it. I am unsure of God's thoughts toward me, but I do not doubt His love for my fellow man, and gladly I tell others of God's unmistakable love for them.

I tell him, "If you are honest, fully confessing your sins and actually sorry for them, then our God will forgive you and your soul will be saved."

My mom has been standing beside me, also looking at Stephen, listening and watching. She now begins to talk to him herself. Bold and clear my steady sidekick says to Stephen, "He who is free in the spirit is free indeed—even behind bars."

Now words and the integrity of hearts are about to be tested. Suddenly, this murderer, Stephen Stewart, stretches out his arm that has been facing us and holds his hand out to me. I look at his hand and then at him and see that his eyes are pleading with me for a touch of compassion. Maybe some sort of reassurance or deliverance from all this? I don't know what he wants or needs.

Chapter Fourteen

Being as we are family, I have many times in the past been physically close to him, as I am with all my kin, without any thought of it, but after what Stephen did to my dad, how he so cruelly made him suffer, even with God's miracle to us here today, I still feel this man to be someone I don't know anymore, and he is scary to me.

I just stand there looking back and forth from his extended hand to his eyes. *Oh, God, please don't make me hold his hand, the hand he held a knife in to kill Dad*, I desperately say in my mind. Looking beyond Stephen, I see that Mr. Askren, his aid, and the deputy are all looking at me along with Stephen still. They are all waiting to see what I will do, and each of them has a different expression on their face. I wonder what my mama is thinking now or what her expression is. I don't know.

All I feel is dread as I hold back my tears, but within me I hear, "Is all that was said and what happened today real or not?" Yes! It was all real and true. So, I step forward and put my hand in his.

DREAMS

Second Dream

Dreamt January 2013

My family and I are at a house that I feel is ours, but it is one we have never lived in before. The house is a simple, open, small but nice ranch-style house with cream-colored siding. The house sits back from the road on a nice-sized piece of property that isn't very wide, but it is deep. From the doorway to the right until the end of the house there is a wide porch, and at the end it has steps that go toward the backyard.

The dream takes place in present time, with Dad having been gone for one year and almost eleven months. In the dream, though, the state has still not yet released my dad to me in order for me to bury him, since the investigation is still going on.

I get a call early Wednesday morning from the D.A.'s office telling me that they are now releasing my dad's body to me, and I am free to bury him. He would be delivered before noon. My husband and the kids are at the house, and I tell them, and we are all very relieved. I call the funeral home and tell them that my dad's body will be arriving later in the day, and we make plans to have the funeral Friday. All the troubles and heartbreak of the past almost two years will be over Friday. Dad will finally be buried, with him and us all being able to rest in peace now.

Second Dream

In the dream, my relief was so overwhelming, so real—all my feelings were. Everything I saw, touched, and smelled was all very real.

It is later in the morning now and a truck from the coroner's office pulls up to the house and unloads a casket from the back of the truck. The men ask me where I want it, but I don't know what to say to them. So, my husband points to the end of the porch, where the steps are to the back. I sign their paper, and they leave like this is how it's supposed to be.

It was the same casket my dad was actually, in real life, buried in.

I open it, and there he is, wearing the same clothes I had him buried in—a long-sleeved dark blue jean dress shirt and dark jeans. I quickly close the casket, and my family and I all look at each other, not knowing what to do now. This is weird. I had expected him to be delivered to a funeral home, not my house. Even though this isn't what I thought would happen, and it is strange, I am still very much relieved and excited. I know where Dad is now. I can take care of him. He is in my possession, and I am now going to be able to finish this for him. He shouldn't have been delivered to my house, though. So, what now? We will just wait until Friday. He will be alright on the porch until his funeral.

We all go back into the house and have a normal rest of the day. When it is late in the evening, just before dark, I hear some noises outside, and so I go and look out the front door. I see a white van that had been backed into the driveway now leaving, and a man runs to catch up to the van. He jumps in through the back door. They quickly turn onto the street and leave.

"What are they up to?" I think. I know something is wrong, and I suddenly feel very anxious. I look to the end of the porch where my dad is supposed to be, but he is gone. Those people stole him from me! He was taken away again, just when I had gotten him back and thought the murder, along with all its trouble, was coming to an end. I am crushed. Not only was he stolen, but so was my hope and healing.

I turn around back into the house and tell my family that my dad was just stolen and we need to call the police. I call the police and tell the dispatcher that a casket was just stolen off my porch. She wants to know why I had a casket at my house, and I tell her that it wasn't just a casket—my dad's body was in there, and he was stolen along with it. Now her tone of voice and attitude with me is that she thinks I'm some kind of weirdo as she asks why I have my dad's body and if I have any other dead bodies at my house.

I sharply tell her, "No, I do not!" I am upset now. I am mad at what she's asking and that she is wasting time asking dumb questions. I explain to the dispatcher that my dad had been murdered almost two years ago and that the state had just released him to me this morning, and I'm sure he was delivered to my house by mistake and that he was going to be buried on Friday.

Her attitude is a little better now toward me, but not totally right. The dispatcher asks me what the casket looks like and then says the thieves were probably just after the casket and didn't realize there was a body in it. She then tells me that when the thieves discover the body they will most likely dump it. She says the officers will be on the lookout for the van I described to her and the casket. I then tell her I don't care anything about the casket. I want my dad's body back. That's all I want. I then tell her what he looks like and what my dad is wearing. The dispatcher tells me the officers will do what they can and let me know what happens. I tell her "Thanks," but I feel like, "Yeah, thanks for nothing."

I go into the kitchen and my husband calls out to me that he is going out. The kids must have left with him, because now I am alone. Thursday comes with no word, and I am still alone. It is now Friday—the day I was supposed to bury Dad, the day I hoped we were both going to be able to rest in peace—yet there is still no news from the police, and I am still alone, though being alone doesn't seem strange.

In the early afternoon I am sweeping the floor when suddenly there is a knock at the front door. The knock is firm against the door, and it startles me. I rest the broom against the kitchen wall and quickly go to the door thinking it might be the police with some information, finally.

I open the door, and, instead of the police, it is my dad standing there. I hold on to the door and just stand there, looking at him. It is actually him, alive, standing there on the front porch. He looks just like he did the last time I saw him alive, just very, very tired. Dad is even wearing the outfit he had been buried in. After a few moments of staring at each other, I say, "Where have you been? I've been looking for you." Dad smiles at me without saying anything and takes a step forward like he wants to come in. So, I step back and hold the door all the way open for him.

Dad comes in, his work boots heavy on the wooden floors. He goes over and sits down on the couch. I go over and stand over him, looking into his eyes and he mine. All the fears and troubles of the past are gone now. He is here. He shouldn't be here or alive, but I don't care how or why. It is like when a mistake is made at the post office in the shipping department; as long as you don't report it, the mistake will not get corrected. He will be my secret, and everything will be alright. He will live here with me, and no one will take him away ever again.

Dad suddenly begins darting his eyes back and forth across the room and then asks, "Where's the kids?" I tell him that they are gone right now. I then kneel down and sit on the floor right at his feet with my hand on his knee. I tell him as he looks down at me that I have missed him and that he has been gone a long time. He looks a little puzzled but doesn't say anything, so I say, "Don't you know what happened? Don't you remember?"

He looks up, then closes his eyes and says, "I remember Jonathon."

I say again, "Don't you remember?"

He says, "I saw Jonathon."

I tell him, "No! It wasn't Jonathon, it was Stephen. Stephen killed you." I am crying now, and he looks down at me and pats my hand. I tell him, "But I prayed for you! God was there."

"I know," he says.

"I prayed for you. Stephen's evil didn't win," I tell him, still crying.

Again, he says, "I know," as he is still patting my hand on his knee. Dad then looks up and says, "My head hurts," almost as a question.

I tell him, "I know." This is not like him to express that something is hurting him or for him to have a headache. We start talking about oddball things. Then he stops again and tells me that his head hurts, but looks right at me this time, and his eyes are sad. I tell him, "Yes, I'm sure your whole body does."

All is quiet as we look at each other, and I know that he knows. In his eyes I can tell he sees his murder, and I feel afraid for him. Dad then blinks his eyes, looks at me and says, "You reckon," with a wink, then he smiles at me, and I smile back, but my heart is breaking for him. Dad now tells me that he is tired and wants to lie down.

I tell him, "No!" with a snap because for some reason I know that if he goes to sleep he will be gone. He does look so tired, though, and sounds tired, too. I feel bad for him, but I don't want him to be gone. He looks at me a little surprised, so I tell him that he has just gotten here, and I don't want him to leave.

He leans forward and says, looking straight into my eyes, "I've come to you. Do you understand?"

I tell him, "Yes," but I don't understand.

He strokes my hair for a moment then leans back against the couch. He looks around the room as he sits there, while I'm studying him, soaking him in, in a way, before he is gone. I know he can't stay.

My dad looks down at me and with an anxious voice tells me that he must go lie down. He gets up without waiting for a response from me and heads toward the bedroom—his bedroom. So, I stand up, and as I am following him, I tell him, "Then I will sit with you." He lies down on top of the bed without getting under the covers or taking his boots off, and I sit on the bed next to him. I hold his arm and tell him again that I've missed him. He is getting sleepy now, but with a firm voice he tells me again, "I've come to you. Do you understand? Do you understand?"

I tell him I don't want him to leave now, because I feel he is going to. Dad just smiles at me as I hold on to his arm. We start talking about different things, but I'm not sure what—just a little bit, though, because he is trying to go to sleep. I am talking to try and keep him awake. All of a sudden, I see a scene playing out before my eyes as though I am seeing it live, and I say out loud, "What is happening?" Dad looks at me and puts his hand on mine. He looks peaceful, but in a way afraid also.

I see two cars driving down one of the back roads in the country in Tennessee with fenced fields along both sides of the road. One field has quite a few pretty thoroughbred horses in it, and the two cars pull alongside the road to stop and get out. These people are friends or family with each other. They cross over the ditch and stand at the fence to look at the horses. They are talking and laughing with each other. Some distance down the road, coming toward the people looking at the horses, is the white van I saw leave my house with Dad's casket.

The van slows down as it comes closer to the people along the road. About fifty feet or so from where the people are is the corner of the pasture and a long driveway to the house of the owners of the property. The van pulls into the driveway and goes a little way up into it. Three men get out of the van, yelling, arguing over the casket. They are angry that the casket is empty and that their boss is going to be mad. They are afraid of what's going to happen to them, so they try to put together their plan. The people at the fence are not sure what's going on and act like they want to leave. The three men notice the people wanting to leave, so they all—no, two of the men, jump over the fence into the pasture and are yelling for the people to get into the pasture too. The people are afraid and back away from the fence.

My dad, with urgency, tells me that he has to go, but I tell him, "No," and he grips my forearm. I go back, almost uncontrollably, reporting what I am seeing. My husband drives past the field and the people. He stops and backs up into the driveway just inside it and stops. He is watching, not knowing what is happening. But he does know the men in the fence are the ones who stole Dad. He'd apparently been looking for them.

The men in the field are still yelling at the people outside to get inside. The people are afraid, but, maybe because they feel they have no choice, they all climb over the fence. The third man who did not get into the pasture goes over to the back of the van, opens it up, and prepares to do what they had planned when they saw the people alongside the road.

In the back is my dad's casket, and the man is unlatching it. The two men in the field are arguing with each other, even though one of them has a gun pointed at the people. There are two women and maybe four men. They are wanting to run, but they are scared. They can hear what the men are arguing about—who to kill. They must pick the right person to replace my dad's body to satisfy their boss. It must be the right person. Finally, they have it narrowed down to one of the women and a man. They separate the two from the group. I see my dad looking at me, even as I see what is playing out.

Dad is wide awake now and says he must go! I don't say anything this time. He smiles at me, and I smile back at him. The man with the gun points it at the one man and fires. My dad is instantly gone, and the bullet never reaches who it was meant for. My dad is back in that casket.

I know that and so do the three men. The two jump the fence back to the van and, without checking in the casket, they latch it back and shut the doors. The three jump into the van and very quickly back out, throwing gravel, never noticing my husband.

As the van turns out of the driveway, I can see my dad's casket through the back door windows, and I can see that my dad is in there. He didn't allow anyone to take his place. The van speeds out of my sight. The people in the field are stunned, but unhurt, and my husband turns in my direction of view and looks as if he is looking at me. He knows I saw it. I saw it all as I sat on my dad's bed that is now empty.

Chapter Fifteen

EVEN WITH THE YEARS that have passed since that day in court, this is still hard for me to think about and write down. I can still feel the touch of Stephen's hand, the repulsive clamminess of his skin. This entire story has been so very difficult and time-consuming for me to write. Most of what is written here comes from the endless notes that were taken over the course of this journey as the experiences were happening or not long after, drawing from memories that were still fresh from each event. It was after this strenuous expedition had come to an end that I then began compiling my notes and heart into a single notebook. Through God's guidance my thoughts and grief began to pour out from me through writing this story while I stood behind a set of bleachers alongside a grassy field. It was there that I would use a bleacher seat at my level for a table, where I would write and cry—while also trying to watch my kids have fun during the homeschooled kids' "Home Team" sports at Silver Spur each Tuesday afternoon.

Now being closer to him in the room, and him having a hold of my hand, makes me feel trapped, fretful, and even a little queasy. This is especially so from being able to smell so strongly the putrid odors from his infected wounds and an amputation. It is true I am not happy standing so close to this man while we hold each other's hands, but I know I am supposed to for some strange reason. And so, I soften my heart before him.

Stephen looks at me and softly says, "Thank you." I look up and see a surprised look on Mr. Askren's face and tears in the eyes of his aid. Mercy, real mercy, can only come from God. Stephen tells my mom and me that he wants us to tell my brother and other family members that he hopes they will be able to forgive him one day. We both say we will. He also tells me that he is glad that I was the one who was here today. I tell him I was glad also and that I have been a part of this from the beginning.

God has helped me so kindly and powerfully in the courtroom today, made His presence known, and made the way for His words to be heard. "Vengeance is Mine," says the Lord (Deut 32:35)—yes, Sir, it is. God ministered to me; I believe He ministered to Stephen, also, and everyone else there, to each in the ways He knew they individually needed. That beautiful form so heavily laden with the presence of God hovering over Stephen earlier was more than just forgiveness—it was the tiniest glimpse of His glory.

The power of God, His truth, and, yes, even justice, are all alive and working in the midst of all this today, and proof is about to be revealed that He really was there from the beginning.

As though sensing that his time is about up, Stephen seems to stall for this last bit of freedom by talking faster about a few oddball things to me. I stop him because there is something I must know before he is taken away to begin his rightly deserved prison sentence.

What I want to ask I do not know the right words for, not then or even now. I say quietly and stumbling over myself, "Stephen, did my dad, did he, did he die, did he die—nicely?" I quickly try to fix my question as I desperately force myself to hold back the tears. "No, not nicely, but did he die—" Stephen stops me, grips my hand tight and pulls it to his chest, pulling the rest of me up against his gurney. Seeing Stephen pull me in closer, those in the room all become more alert, as though they may have to intervene.

Understand, I know all the details of how my dad died. I walked through his fire- and smoke-damaged house. I saw where my dad was standing at his kitchen counter having what would be his last meal. I saw the cooking pot dented in and bloodied from being used to hit him in the back of the head when Stephen came up behind him. I saw my dad's recognizable handprint and finger smears made in his own blood as he picked himself up off of the kitchen floor. I saw the back of Dad's recliner in the living room stained from his bloodied head, with his cell phone opened, lying on the floor next to his chair. I saw all the blood—my dad's blood—splattered and smeared throughout the room and the imprints left by him in each blood-soaked area where he went down and then got back up again as he fought for his life, trying to hold back the murderer's knife. I saw where my dad's life, his spirit, left his body, which was deeply stabbed and sliced several dozens of times then nearly beheaded. Stephen then attempted to burn my dad's body to cover up the evidence, but his body did not burn. I was the one who dealt with and saw, smelt, held, and heard all the reports, investigations, pictures, evidence, and autopsy statements. Do you see, I know!

I am the one who has been submerged in the filth of it all, trudging through to do what had to be done, and forever the horrors of all that will be a part of me. But, thankfully, not only the horrors will forever be with me, but also the honor of God allowing me to work for my dad and Him. Not only brutality and pure evil did I experience from many things and people throughout all of this—I also experienced God's protection and guidance, gentleness, and even joy.

So now, at the end of it all, this murderer who had drawn me up close while holding my hand was about to be compassionate toward me.

Stephen puts his other hand over both of ours against his chest as he interrupts my stutterings that came from not knowing how to put into words what I want to ask him. I close my mouth and look at him through the tears in my eyes and he says, soothingly, "I don't remember everything that happened during that, but I do remember, before it was over, that your dad said, 'I forgive you.'"

My mama responds in either disbelief or awe and says, "If Junior did say that, then. . ." Stephen, visibly irritated, quickly interrupts, "Junior did say that he forgives me, and I hope he meant it." I just stand there, staring at him with an overwhelming feeling of love, pride, and relief for my truly amazing dad. I only quietly respond out loud by saying that I know that he did. My dad spoke what he meant. Stephen lets out a breath and is noticeably relieved and then lets go of my hand.

With the release of my hand, I step back, away from the gurney and Stephen. I don't know what to say now to him, but I want to run out that open door screaming, "Thank you, God!" I knew, honestly, I knew that Jesus was there with my dad by his side from the midnight hours of when I was awoken by Him to pray until later that afternoon when my dad's life ended. God Almighty was there with Dad. He was not alone. So, with what Stephen just revealed to me and knowing the kind of man my dad was, I have no doubt he stayed true to his character and allowed God's nature and reality to be revealed. Even as his life was being brutally taken.

When dad had said he knew God was real, he was right. Junior Taylor knew his God, and God knew him. The act of my dad telling the man who was violently trying to end his life for no reason except greed, in the very midst of it, or even with his last breath, that he forgave him could have only come from God and proves to me that our Lord was there.

I am so proud of my dad, my beloved father and friend who truly understood me and loved me. This man proved time and again his whole life he was a hard worker and heroic in every sense of the word, showing what his heart was made of. He strived hard to fix and overcome the sins of his past to become the man he was. With persistence he pushed; relentlessly he called me not to repeat his own mistakes and not to be of this world.

Junior Taylor was a fighter—in more ways than one. He was a sinner, a repenter, one who struggled, yet he was redeemed and saved. There was no one else like him. His entire life was full of hardships, either caused by others or by his own means, and he was tormented by things he had seen, been taught, and was a part of as a child and later in life, things that many could never understand or even imagine. But without a doubt, this man, my dad, was

Chapter Fifteen

an overcomer, and during his 55 years on this earth, he lived his life to its fullest and made a profound impact upon people's lives along the way, especially mine—all the way up to the end.

Chapter Sixteen

OUR TIME HERE AT the county courthouse is drawing to a close. If one was to look at this building as they drove past this afternoon, I doubt they could have even imagined the remarkable events that have been occurring here today.

Stephen now tells my mom and me that he may never come out of the prison he is going to. I only reply flatly with, "I know."

Mom says, "Remember that he who is free in the spirit is free indeed" (referencing John 8:36). Stephen then says in a desperate way how he will probably die there in that prison. I tell him that with whatever time he has left and wherever he is at, to use it for good, that there is still a purpose for him. "Give your life to God, look for ways to help those you can, and be thankful," I tell him.

The man who has hurt so many people and has made such a devastating mess of his life, within moments from beginning his prison sentence, now smiles at my mom and me with his whole countenance brightening up. He says to us that he will try to do what we said and that maybe he can help others.

My mama and I both give a slight smile back at Stephen with a nod. I thank him for saying what he had and again for agreeing to make this happen today. "It's meant a lot to me," I tell him, and I say goodbye. Mom now quickly cups her hands over his and tells him goodbye also. We then turn together and leave the room, closing the door behind us.

With the closing of that door I know my God-ordained mission has come to an end. In that uninviting, stale room there was no glitter or fanfare, no ticket parade to celebrate or even take

Chapter Sixteen

notice of my completion of this journey that has seemed to have no end. Yet, quietly in there it has come to an end, the trail gate has finally been pulled shut, and the last lines of the closing act have been read, freeing me at last from my evil travel partner.

Jesus commands us to pick up our cross and follow Him; even if the road is treacherous we must step forward. This route chosen for me and what I carried along the way was ugly alright, and certainly not pleasant, but if I had not chosen to pick up this cross, what I was called out to do, the road of disobedience would have been far worse than what I experienced down this particular path.

Stephen did die in prison, May 6, 2018, at 45 years old, from causes which stemmed from the lasting effects of his attempted suicide the night of the murder. I instantly felt a sense of relief when the district attorney's office called to tell me he had died. I was then troubled with myself the next couple of days, as though I was wrong or had no right to be feeling such a way. I always felt he deserved his punishment and worse for murdering my father, but I never wished Stephen dead.

Out the courtroom doors my faithful supporter and I go, her holding on to my arm as though she senses my strength fading. Maybe hers, too?

Through the doors and into the hallway, I, without stopping, make my way to the restrooms just a little further down. I head straight to the sink once inside. I pump lots and lots and even more soap onto my hands, scrubbing them and my arms thoroughly, repeatedly under the hot water of the faucet. I have to wash Stephen off of me. I want the feel of his hands, his smell, all the horrors and heartache he has put me through for the past two-and-a-half years to all be washed away!

This need to wash is also because I have been assaulted and harassed by men over the years, where I've had to physically do what I could to free myself from them. I hated the feel of their unwanted hands and body on mine, against my skin, and being able to smell them on myself. I have to get the feeling of Stephen's hands off of mine. The filth of all the evil that has happened I want washed away. So I keep scrubbing.

I have wondered, even worried, that my determined efforts there at that sink to wash the feel of my dad's murderer off my hands makes me some type of hypocrite in regards to what God did in me today. My heart and words, my willingness for God's will to be done in all this was and is sincere. I hope you can understand.

Mom stands a couple of feet away from me, holding out paper towels as a suggestion for me to finish. She says in her motherly tone, "Hoppy, it's okay; it is all over with now."

I turn off the water and am exhausted. I take the paper towels from Mom and just want to sit on the floor and cry. Mom takes my hand and says we are leaving now. I see she is also drained from all that has happened.

Through the halls of the courthouse and out the doors she and I go together without looking back.

As we are walking to our car, Stephen's sister and her husband come up alongside of us. She is sad, but also relieved. She and her husband both are kind and friendly to us and thank my mom and me for how everything was handled and what was said.

I don't know if she was ever given the chance to speak with her brother when the legal formalities were over. Maybe before he was taken into the holding room while I was talking to the judge and Ms. West? I hope so. We all talk a bit and then hug each other goodbye, wishing one another the best as we go our separate ways after such an eventful day.

Laura and her husband leave the parking lot and head back to Alabama. Mama and I wave as they pass. Our day is not over yet, either, for now we know we have to go find my brother and tell him what has happened.

My brother does not know anything about this court date, the plea deal, or even that Mom and I are in town. There is much he has not known all the way from the beginning. He is not going to be happy that he has been kept in the dark about today. But this is how I knew it had to be, and I am not sorry for my choices of keeping him uninvolved in this entire process. I have no regrets or shame in how I handled myself or this quest I was put on. I can rest in that fact.

Chapter Seventeen

It's over, it's really over after all this time. Can you believe it? I made it over the finish line alive and intact spiritually and emotionally. I am utterly exhausted from such a long, strenuous journey. But I got the job done, and the end of it all was far more beautiful than I could have ever imagined. God is amazing. Our journey ended with victory, glorious victory. I am truly blessed and honored to have been called for such a time as this.

When I was seventeen years old, I was in a traumatic auto accident. I was not a Christian. I did not know God, nor was I ever taught the truth of His Word. As my body smashed into the front of a car from being hit head-on while on a moped, I met my Maker. This is an entirely different story, and I won't go into it much, but I will tell you that I learned Jesus, our God, Lord, Creator of all, and yes, Savior, is real.

My body was severely damaged from the multiple life-threatening injuries I received. After five months in a hospital and numerous surgeries, my body mended, but it was never the same.

It was my soul and spirit that changed the most, though, and forever I will be thankful for that experience, even with all the lasting pain, additional surgeries, and troubles. It has been worth it all.

Through that extreme experience of mine, I learned from the Great Teacher Himself that there is no other God but Him, and heaven is real also, along with hell. I stood in the presence, the actual literal presence, of the one and only true living God in a place that was nothing of this world we know. I entered the room to where He was at through an enormous marble-looking door that

Chapter Seventeen

was partly open, as if I were expected and welcomed, whereas all the doors behind me were closed. In there, standing before our God, I felt His power, heard His voice, saw His form and glory, along with His angels. I absolutely know my God is real. It is true, as it says in the Bible, that every knee will bow and every tongue will confess that Jesus is Lord (Phil 2:10–11). It's best to do it now while you still can—you may not get a second chance.

I am alive only because of God, for medically there was no hope. I have the ability to walk, bear children, and do all I can only by God's power and mercy. My many scars are ugly, and I am not much to look at on the outside, but what God has done within me is beautiful. He is the true definition of beauty.

While I was standing before Him, Jesus asked me if I wanted to live or die. I answered Him by saying that I wanted to live. Our all-powerful God simply said, "All right then."

Since that time, I have known, truly known, that Jesus, the Creator of all heaven and Earth, the God of the Bible, is real, and over and over He has continued to reveal this fact to me along with the truth of His Word.

Once again, today, He has done that for me, but not just for me. Jesus has revealed Himself to everyone in that courtroom. Did they open their hearts, their understanding, and receive Him, or did they turn a blind eye?

It has been a long day. So much has happened. Needing a moment for ourselves, my mom and I decide to stop at a restaurant to settle our minds and gain some strength back before talking to my brother, which we expect will be an exhausting chore in itself.

We sit in a booth at what happens to be the same restaurant I was at only a couple weeks earlier, where I was given a piece of pie by a kind waitress. Mom says we need to write down what happened in that courtroom, things that were said, because it was so unbelievable. I find a small notebook in my purse, and she takes notes as we both empty out our thoughts and hearts about what has happened. We are in awe, excited, drained, relieved, and even heartbroken, but grateful—so very grateful to God for what He has done.

After all the notes are taken and our teas drunk, we leave to go find my brother. There's no telling where he might be, but we decide his house is the best place to start our search. He actually is living on what was our dad's property, which I gave him along with all the means necessary to have a new manufactured home to replace Dad's. And here it is where we do find Brother and his family. They are all shocked to see us when we come to the door.

I was the one who made the decision to keep my brother and anyone else I could from knowing about the agreed-upon plea deal and court date. I had let my firm decision of this desire for secrecy be known of course to the D.A.'s team, but besides them it was only my mom, the kids, and my husband who knew about this plea deal with its court date. Since I was the one who had kept my brother and the rest of the family out of the courtroom today, I need to be the one to speak up first and confess what I have done. I ask him to come outside with me alone so I can talk to him uninterrupted.

Of course, my brother is mad. He paces back and forth outside on the large concrete-slab porch where our dad enjoyed "eatin' and visitin'" with folks, as he would say, when he was home. As he's pacing I try to explain what happened today at the county courthouse and why I chose to keep him out of this and out of many of the other things I did surrounding the loss of our father. This was no longer Dad's home, and the property looked different than it did when he lived here, but, maybe out of habit, I couldn't help glancing around expecting—hoping—to see him as I was having difficulty talking to my older brother.

From the beginning, there was much for me to weigh out and consider when it came to my decision in how involved or in-the-know my brother or others would be of all that pertained to this case. A major factor that played a part in this decision was the fact that several officials from different agencies made it clear to me they did not want to have any communications with my brother or his wife. Also, I knew my brother could not handle the stress, the grief, or the workload from our dad's tragic death. I have always loved him and have done what I can to help my brother and his family, but I too often only received bitterness and blame from my brother in return for my help when he suffered the results of their drug use and other poor choices.

So, for many reasons, I did not want my brother, any of our family, or even the public in that courtroom today. I wanted my God to have His way in there. It was God, my dad, and me in the beginning of all this, starting with that midnight prayer, and I needed it to be just us there in the end, with my mom stepping in on behalf of Dad. It could only have been her to stand in his place next to me.

Yes, my brother is mad, along with his family. It is very tense, with foul language and frustrations, and I imagine hurt, too, from their side. I am not sorry for my decision, and I do not back down from it, but I try to be understanding toward them and show them that I do care about them. My mom does what she can, acting as a referee. Finally, at the end of our time talking together, during which it had seemed as though nothing I was trying to explain had gotten through, my brother now calmly tells me he knows he couldn't have handled what went on today or the many other things I had to do after our dad was killed. To my surprise, he then, in a way, thanks me for handling it all.

You, also, may think I was selfish or controlling to keep the court date to myself. I know that there were far more people beyond just myself who loved my dad and missed him, needed a feeling, a sense of closure and healing from his tragic end, too. Believe me, I know others have been hurting, that they were struggling with anger, unforgiveness, and loss.

My own children who are so dear to me were a part of all this also. They were with me on trips I took driving to Tennessee to take care of business. Sadly, my kids knew too much at their young ages of the evils of this world firsthand. They heard me up in the wee hours of the mornings for the previous two-and-a-half years, making the necessary phone calls to different officials or receiving at odd times those calls of harassment and pleas for help. There were endless stacks of paperwork I had to complete in order to finalize all matters my dad had his name to. In between homeschooling lessons and houses to clean, I would regularly drive down to a local mail and print shop. I did not own a fax machine but very much needed one for all the out-of-state business I was doing. Much time was spent sitting on the floor with my back against the wall near the far counter of this peaceful little shop, waiting for scheduled faxes to come in. I would sit there, often with the owner's teddy-bear-of-a-dog lying beside me, as I read the various documents that came in and filled out what I needed to; then I'd hand the papers back up to the worker at the counter to fax them back.

I did want my kids to have that sense of closure they might have needed that may have come about by being in the courtroom today. I, as a mother, didn't want them to hear the things that would be said or to see Stephen, but I still carried guilt and hurt for them because they were unable to go to their Papa's funeral. But if they came to this proceeding then I was afraid that my husband would feel he also would have the right to be there. Just as with my brother, my husband also, and him being the way he is, to have him in that courtroom was an option I absolutely would not consider. Travis, Jacob, and HannahGrace understood that.

I did not act out of selfishness, arrogance, or a desire to hurt anyone, but only with a will to let God do what He had planned to do without hindrances or a circus show being made out of this day. I needed to see this thing through until the end with the spotlight on God—not on others who didn't understand.

Dad had entrusted me, not my brother or anyone else, to take care of whatever had to be done for him. Outside one snowy morning not long before he left us all, I promised my dad that I would do what he was asking of me. I promised and so I did it all, the best I could, to the very end. I hope somehow he knows that.

This makes me think about all those sweet and funny memories I have of the fantastic stories Dad would call and tell me to keep himself awake when he'd get sleepy while driving (he averaged

Chapter Seventeen

1,200 miles a day). My dad would make up story after story of a messy-headed fairy he had who helped him, and of his magic house that did his chores for him while he was out on the road. Over time the saga would grow in complexity with new, elaborate adventures for this fairy of his. Dad never gave her an actual name (besides "Messy-Headed"), but it was me he was portraying in those stories—my dad would make that clear even without coming right out and saying it. The messy hair reference of course gave it away, plus a time or two he'd slip and call the fairy Girlie, which is one of the names he had for me. I honestly cannot recall a time in my life when my dad called me by my real name.

I know, of course, Dad would have handled the job of this load much better than I have. He was tough alright and would do what had to be done until it was done, without fear or difficulties guiding him. Pain did not stop my dad. Sometimes I would tease him about this, saying that if he ever got his arm whacked off, he'd just put duct tape around it, ask me to hand him his coffee, then continue on with whatever job he was doing. Dad would just smile and say, "Ya reckon?" then wink at me. That was pert near what happened too, when he cut off the tip ends of a few fingers in a Skilsaw accident.

Because of the relationship I had with my dad, I had a different role in this whole matter, in his life, than others did. I am not ashamed, nor do I feel a need to justify my actions beyond the ways I have done here. I was true to both my heavenly and earthly fathers, and that is what matters most. Maybe Dad gave Mom and me a wink when we walked out of the courthouse today when it was all over?

Throughout this incredible journey, this unimaginable experience, I have been doubted, ridiculed, criticized, and treated badly by many. But it doesn't matter, for I know I kept my promise.

> In this you greatly rejoice, though now for a little while, if need be, you have been grieved by various trials, that the genuineness of your faith, being much more precious than gold that perishes, though it is tested by fire, may

be found to praise, honor, and glory at the revelation of Jesus Christ. (1 Pet 1:6–7)

Chapter Eighteen

Over the next few days, while my mom spends time with my brother, I wrap up what I need to at the district attorney's office, at the courthouse, with officers, and for all the other legal matters I am responsible for. When my dad wanted me to promise him I would take care of whatever needed to be handled for him when he died, I could not have then imagined what was to be required of me. But at the end of it all, each came together, just as it ought.

God and His truth kept working, spreading among the people and ministering into their hearts after I closed my mouth and walked out those doors, just as He ought.

When deeds or words are of man, they fall apart, are forgotten, and end when the act is done. But, when something is of God, it is alive. It grows and continues on after the work is done. Its effects are lasting. That is how we know if something has come from man or God.

During the past two-and-a-half years of prosecution investigations, I barely saw, heard, or even spoke to the formidable, elected district attorney general for that region. Whether in person or over the phone, it was primarily his colleagues I communicated with when taking care of the matters I had to. But a couple of days after that incredible experience in the courthouse, D.A. General Mickey Layne calls me into his office. I sit down, not knowing what to expect. This highly respected man just comes right out and tells me that a lot of people are talking about what happened in that courtroom during the plea deal. He tells me that no one had ever seen anything like that, and it is hard to believe. I say to him how it really was amazing and turned out far better than I ever had hoped for.

"It was all God's doing," I say. He says that he doesn't know what will come of it, but people are talking. "People are talking," he keeps saying, and he tells me it was a privilege to have worked with me. I tell him I am glad and feel the same way about him and everyone in his office. Each one of those people—along with the many officers; court clerks; another attorney, Mr. Bell; bank officials; and, too, those working on the sidelines helping these people—I have been honored to get to know and work with. They are all incredibly gifted, compassionate people whom God is using in this troubled world. I will forever hold them in my heart, knowing how special they are and how hard they work helping victims of crime and their families, beyond just the realms of the law. They never stopped me from voicing my heartache, frustrations, concerns, or my strong beliefs in who my God is, which meant more to me than I'm sure they realized.

I then tell Mr. Layne God will do what He wants with what happened in that courtroom and all along. The proof that God was continuing to work in the hearts and lives of those who witnessed what He'd done, along with those who heard of what He did, was in the phone calls and cards I received long after that day, including from Stephen while in prison.

From beginning to end God did have a plan, an ultimate purpose in all this, and it was for good and not evil. My dad, Junior Clay Taylor, did not die in vain, nor was our work for naught—"My brethren, count it all joy when you fall into various trials" (Jas 1:2).

I don't know why my dad's life had to end so violently. God Almighty, who is greater and mightier than anything, was with Dad as Stephen allowed himself to be a tool of the devil. God could have stopped Stephen, stopped the devil from his plans devised in hell, but He didn't. I have wondered: Taking into account who our God is, why was my dad murdered, and in such a horrific way? We all have questioned why God allows so much suffering and evil in

Chapter Eighteen

this world—some people even blame God for it. The bill of sale, though, will not be found on Him for all the madness that circles the Earth. Sin, which was created by the devil in the beginning, is still running wild today, being the true cause of all the heartache and devastation in our lives. But through Jesus, God provides a way of escape, healing, salvation, and hope that no one can take away.

> Therefore submit to God. Resist the devil and he will flee from you. Draw near to God and He will draw near to you. (Jas 4:7–8)

Chapter Nineteen

Now, what about that question God asked me when He woke me on the eve of Dad's death? The question my Lord asked was, "Would you be thankful no matter what?" I answered Him, "Yes, I will"—and I meant it. Through it all, from that moment and still today, years later, I have not forgotten. Like then, while in the midst of it, I am continuing to live out what I promised.

I am a quiet person who listens and watches, taking things in, doing what needs to be done. I hold a lot of my emotions and thoughts in, which isn't always good. I don't express physical or emotional pain much. I deal with what I can on my own and the rest I push aside. I am not heartless or uncaring; I have learned to survive. I've had to. And only because of God's mercy I have survived.

I do not trust people easily, and opening my heart like I've done in this story is not something I normally do. And so, because I have, it is important to me that I be honest in who I am—good and bad alike.

I did not ask or volunteer myself to be involved in all the legal, investigative matters of my dad's murder. The police came to me asking for my help and involvement, and because of my promise to Dad, I agreed. I was put to work right away. Not only with the murder case, but also with all the business and personal matters of my dad's that had to be taken care of.

There was no time for me to grieve, to cry, or to sit and reason through such loss in my heart. It is true, by the world's standards I did not go through the grieving process needed in order to heal.

Chapter Nineteen

It was God who was healing me, and by His strength I made it to the other side.

For two-and-a-half years I was bombarded with all the tasks and the evil surrounding my dad's final affairs, along with the selfish, tormenting demands and absurd expectations put on me by many. On top of being a homeschooling mother of three, which was difficult by itself, I cleaned people's houses for a living. I was also dealing with an alcoholic, abusive husband who worked hard at trying to finish out the world's efforts in destroying me completely, inside and out. But I was not alone, even though at times it felt like I was. It really was God Himself who was healing me, helping me through it all.

Never did I let a day go by then or now where I don't sincerely tell my Savoir what I am thankful for.

I am thankful to have had a dad I could respect, love, and look up to. One I could freely talk with, laugh with—he protected me from what he knew of in my life. The abuse from my husband was not known to him. It was the one thing I couldn't tell him, for reasons other abuse victims can understand. I believe he suspected it, but not the severity of it all.

I am grateful my dad took the time to teach my kids and me all he could. He loved us and was a part of us. My dad and I were very much alike personality-wise and so were our views of God, politics, family, and our determination. So it was easy for us to talk, for we understood one another. But there were times we disagreed, and we definitely let each other know we did. I miss having him in my life. We were, as they say, knitted together, and we were glad to be. Yet in that courtroom, when our God allowed me to experience what true forgiveness is meant to be, my dad was also of those I forgave. We had grown close over the years, and I loved him dearly, but this was not always so between us when I was a child. He had admitted his wrongs to me and apologized, but there were still tender, festering wounds deep within me that I harbored of sorrow and hurt my beloved father had inflicted upon me during my younger years. I thank God for second chances on both our parts.

The Final Word

    I am thankful for the influence my dad had come to have on my faith. He would tell me that a Christian life was hard. My dad would say how it demanded more from you than running with the world does. Yet, he believed it was worth it, that God was worth our efforts. As you can imagine, it meant a lot to me when my dad would tell me he was proud of me as a Christian and for being someone who stood on what I believed. To have had someone who was united with me, to have that fellowship with someone who believes in God the way I do, sees Him and His Word for what it is, and not what many others try to make Him or His truth into, is a priceless gift. I so miss having someone I can talk to who truly understands where I come from and what I believe.

    My dad, like myself, was strongly against the unbiblical doctrines of those "name it and claim it" prosperity gospels preached across the lands. Dad would get angry and disgusted by these sugarcoated, poisonous lies and by those who taught them.

    I am thankful for the sincerity of Dad's encouragement to me, his support of my convictions and my commitment to our God.

    I am thankful for the people God put in my dad's life here and there who encouraged him along the way as he made his way to Him. My dad would share with me what he saw, heard, and experienced within himself and what was shared by others who held true to God and His Word. Dad's heart for his God and the respect he had for sincere Christians were sure.

    During Junior Taylor's life there were many men and women alike who thought they were his friends, thought they knew him; but they didn't know him for who he really was and only saw what they wanted from him. I am thankful for the few people who were truly my dad's friends and for those family members whom he did love and appreciate. I am thankful for the friendships I have gained from those genuine friends of his. They, and a few in our family, are a blessing to me.

    I am honestly thankful that I am the one in our family to carry within me the dreadful images along with what had to be heard and those things that had to be done—all so my kids or other family members wouldn't have to live with those things in their hearts or minds. Knowing they are free from that brings me peace.

I am without a doubt thankful for each of my children whom my dad, their papa, had been so proud of.

I am thankful for my dear mama and her unending love, her laughter, and steady hand. She also is one I look up to, respect, and hold dear.

I am thankful for the power of forgiveness, which God so beautifully and profoundly taught me. Through that gift I am able to freely and completely forgive my husband who abused, betrayed, and hurt me in every way possible our entire marriage, which is now over. I do sincerely wish him only the best. I amazingly have no ill will toward him. There is good in him, and I am thankful to be able to see it.

I forgive all those who maliciously came against my children and me with their lies, cruelty, and vandalism. Many have hurt us however they could, justifying themselves under their own banner of Christianity when I finally had the courage to make the abuse in my marriage known. During all the years of abuse I suffered and the traumatic ways he caused us to live, my no-longer husband made sure no one, not anyone knew. So, it was hard for others to believe. Yet, sadly, it is common for those who have been abused to be unfairly punished and kicked when they are already down. People willingly accepted their own false assumptions and lies about me and my life. If they had only just asked me for themselves, they would've learned the truth then and of what is being said still today.

I also forgive a man who continuously treated me so terribly when I was younger, and God knows of all that person has heartlessly stolen from me. But I will not return his obscene, deceitful evil with evil; instead, because of forgiveness, I have been willingly able to serve him during his time of debility.

My brother, along with other family members and strangers alike who have hurt me, causing much difficulty and sorrow in my life throughout this journey and beyond, I too forgive.

Praise to our Lord, for He is God, and we are not!

Thank You, Jesus, for the measure of faith You have given to those who believe and have given their hearts to You. Thank You for Your mercy. Help us to remember and live by Your words: "If My people who are called by My name will humble themselves, and pray and seek My face, and turn from their wicked ways, then I will hear from heaven, and will forgive their sin and heal their land" (2 Chr 7:14).

Thank you, Lord, for the salvation, healing, and hope that can come only through You.

I am humbled with gratitude, for my God has given me a voice here. He has opened the door for me to speak, releasing what is in my heart and making the way for more healing. Through being silenced by the wills of others in my life, I was shackled to the fears, hurt, and even the anger I had within me, caused by the acts of some. It was not only my husband who barred me shut, but others, too.

To be made to feel ashamed and at fault for someone else's actions, to have those you reach out to refuse to listen or even acknowledge the truth of your wounds, is as cutting as the wrongs committed. You may also have those doors, along with the doors to others' hearts and that needed trust, slammed in your face or refusals for those doors to even be opened to you at all. If you have been unheard, unseen, made to feel worthless—hear this! You are important. You are needed. You and your life do matter. You are worth being heard, worth being seen. Yes, you are worthy of being loved and protected.

The Lord of all heaven and Earth does see you and is working on your behalf. Don't be the one who closes your door to Him. "Behold, I [Jesus] stand at the door and knock. If anyone hears My voice and opens the door, I will come in to him and dine with him, and he with Me" (Rev 3:20).

Forgiveness is one of the keys needed to release us from locked doors of hopelessness and despair. People, yes, even those we love, may have stood alongside, rallied with our enemies while we were silenced and afraid, making us feel weak and alone. But

Chapter Nineteen

"He [Jesus] who is in you is greater than he [the enemy] who is in the world" (1 John 4:4). Through that truth we are stronger than we realize. We are overcomers and we will never be silenced again.

God, I am so thankful to You for Your invaluable help to me in writing this story. May it honor both You and my dad.

Amazingly, I am willing and able to still see good in this world and in others. I am still able to love and forgive. That is God! He is amazing and I am just completely awestruck for who God is, what He is, and all the incredible things He in His infinite wisdom has taught me, which my sons also gleaned from, as seen in how they faithfully live their lives in His truth.

Jesus, You are the Great I Am!

As this story is winding down, I say through a released sigh of contentment: He called me out of the darkness for a purpose, and He did not leave me. In all my troubles, fears, and questionings, which have been many, my God has not forsaken me. He held me up and gave me strength to do what I was called to do. I was not perfect, but He was patient and kind.

Thank you, Lord, that I am alive today. I am not lost or destroyed.

Yes, God, I will be thankful no matter what.

The Final Word

| Sonora, CA, during Steve's visit in summer 2023 | Jenny and Steve (Oct.16, 1974–Sept. 11, 2023) |

My brother, Steve, after a miraculous and incredibly personal encounter with the Lord Himself during the summer of 2023, fullheartedly gave his heart to our Savior. He humbly, with sincerity, repented of his sins and reconciled to all of us, his family. We will forever be proud of him for having the courage to acknowledge the state he had been living in for so long, laying it all down and surrendering to God. I love you, big brother.

Chapter Twenty

WELL, THERE YOU HAVE it. All that I have written here is true and unbridled. I have opened my heart and poured myself out, but even more so, God's amazing power and mercy have been exposed throughout this story.

The murder of my father and all that came with it has not been the only difficult thing I have gone through in my life. Throughout my years I have faced many acts of pure evil, heartbreaking struggles, and all-out literal fights just to survive where, at times, I almost didn't make it. My life has never been easy, but no one's is, and we all must face the cruelty of the devil and the consequences of our choices in this lifetime.

There have been times during this incredible story, even here, now, and at times in my past, especially when it has come to my children, where I have been nearly broken. There have been points in my life where within myself I was in a place of such despair, terribly afraid, lonely, done with myself, and doubting who I am. Giving up is easy; there was a moment in my life when I was going to remove myself from the world, but there at the end of Turkey Creek Boat Dock Road God once again came to save me. The only way I am able to live, want to live, and step forward is by not letting go of God. Often it takes all I've got just to hold on to my faith and Him, but I desperately hold on.

Yes, you too must rise up and fight to hold on to our Savior—never let go. He is worth it all.

I do not doubt who my God is, His power, or His goodness—I can't. But trust is a hard thing, especially trusting in what is beyond our sights. This is a real struggle for me, which I repent of often, for I know what God has done during this time of all that is written and so many other times in my life.

The Bible says that His ways are not our ways, His plans are not our plans, and that has proved to be true throughout history. The proof is also there showing that God gives us what it takes to get the job done no matter what. He has done it here for me, and I hope you also have experienced this to be true in your life.

Most assuredly, I am not perfect in any way. I have made plenty of stupid mistakes and outright sinned all throughout my years. Regrettably, I also have so often failed in life, shamelessly disgracing the gifts I was given, sinning against my God, other people, and myself. Repetitively sorrowful I am of my sins and the hurt I have caused. Yet when I do sin, so undeservedly I am forgiven by the Savior of our souls who continually sets me back on my feet. Being a Christian, yes, a repentant, bought-by-the-blood-of-Jesus Christian, is what has changed my heart and way of thinking. Since that moment of coming face-to-face with my wretched self and then giving my heart to God, I have willingly tried to push forward and live for Him. Once we make that choice to become a Christian, our lives are called to be different.

Because of Jesus, we are able to endure the trials of this world. We all are able to overcome and push through the devil's snares as long as we hold true to God. Remember to never give up. Never stop loving. Never stop forgiving. Be thankful in all things! Don't forget your past, but always keep moving forward with your eyes set ahead.

My children whom I truly do love, I wrote this story for you, but God wanted it for others also. So to all I say, you are precious, cherished, wanted, and appreciated by your loved ones and even more so by God. Again I say to you: you and your life are worth far more than you realize. Jesus, who is God, is not a myth or legend, and so the only way for salvation and heaven is by surrendering to Him and accepting the sacrifice He made for you. He is reaching out to you; grab hold of Him and never let go. Saying you are a Christian is one thing, but living it out is another and tests our hearts. Our words and actions, how we live our lives, reveal our true hearts and who or what it is we really worship.

I do believe that, no matter what, our God is on the throne. He is not absent or uninvolved. Humanity and His creation is important to Him in both life and death. He sees the tears fall, the blood that is shed, a surrendered heart, and the acts of rebellion. Even when we do not understand, He has a plan. My dearly missed father's life and, as difficult as it is to say, his death, too, was for a reason.

In this chapter added to my family's book of life, we experienced how the devil worked hard to destroy my dad, who God is, and my faith, but he did not win. Lies, heartache, time, and the evidence of evil to cause doubt were stacked against us. At times there seemed to be no way out, no way for the truth of God and the reality of what happened to be brought into the light. Did the devil get so caught up in the excitement of the brutality and hardships of this case, thinking he might win, that he forgot the most important factor? God cannot be overcome or destroyed. The Lord's truth and our faith that good does come to those who put their trust and hope in Him was not wasted. The devil has no power over God or His will no matter what may be thrown at Him or stacked against us.

Yes, it is true the devil does come to steal, kill, and destroy. Sadly, in this case, in our story here, laws, hearts, and lives were broken. The sorrow was great, but God is greater, and it was not the end. So, as you see, it is not the physical evidence or skills of the attorneys that close a case. The devil does not have the final word in our lives or souls. God can and does resurrect life, hope, and healing out of the ashes.

May we all strive to say: "I have fought the good fight, I have finished the race, I have kept the faith" (2 Tim 4:7).

DREAMS

Third Dream

Dreamt May 2017

This dream plays out in the present time. It has been six years now that my dad has been gone. A lot has happened. All the murder business is over, two of my children have graduated high school, leaving HannahGrace left only to homeschool. Also, my husband and I are separated—have been for a year now after I finally had the courage to say "no more" to his abuse and destructive behaviors.

There is a knock on my door early one morning where my kids and I share a home in Confidence. I open the front door and there, standing before me, is my dad. Without either one of us saying a word, I throw myself into his arms, not caring that he shouldn't be here. Dad hugs me tight in his strong arms. He is sound, healthy, well in all ways. He smells good and he's warm. With my head against his chest all my loneliness and pain melt away.

Dad lets me go and I step back, holding the door open for him. He does not come into the house but tells me he wants the kids and I to take a walk with him.

I call the kids over. When they see their Papa, they are instantly excited and go to him without any hesitations and all smiles. My dad returns their excitement and smiles with a big smile of his own and extends his arms out to gather the three of them up, but then the kids'

Third Dream

smiles and excitement of having their Papa with them like old times quickly turns to looks of confusion and even fear. Dad sees this and, while he looks directly at each one of them, he soothingly and quietly tells Travis, Jacob, and HannahGrace that it's okay, and he gently strokes the sides of their cheeks with his big, rough, working hands.

Dad looks up from the kids and says that we all need to put our shoes on and get long-sleeved shirts, because we are going to take a walk with him now. None of us asks questions. We just do as he says. We all go out, and I shut the door behind me.

In a line, we follow him down the stairs and out of the driveway. I see my dad notice his truck parked in the driveway, and he gives me a nod. Up the road we head with Dad still in the lead and the rest of us bunched up behind him. Dad doesn't say anything, but I can tell he knows where he is going and is on some sort of mission.

We follow him out to the end of Confidence South Fork. He turns left onto the highway, and we line up directly behind him. I watch his long strides and listen to the sound of his work boots on these rough mountain roads. I have missed the sound of his voice and laughter, the sound of his boots as he walks. I have missed the way he smells, the look of his large, scarred-up, engine-grease-stained hands that were a symbol of safety and love to me. I watch my dad as he walks in front of me, taking it all in before he's gone, because I know this time he won't last.

Being led by Dad, we cross over the Sierras, always walking in a single-file line; we continuously walk, never stopping. Over mountains, through valleys, wide open plains, and forests we steadily walk.

None of us grows tired or hungry, neither cold nor afraid. The kids and I don't know where we are going or when our journey will end. We trust Dad and are at peace as we follow him.

Days and nights come and go, but I cannot tell you how many. While we steadily walk, we are talking to each other, laughing and enjoying being together. He turns his head toward us, smiling, giving us a wink or a silly expression, as he tells stories. Sometimes we see other people or cars, but never do we talk to anyone else, and people do not acknowledge us.

The Final Word

Dad has been protective of us all, but he is also very lighthearted and peaceful. We all are. As we come out of a field and onto a narrow straight, Dad, and the whole feeling of our journey, changes.

Dad is now serious and reaches for my hand. When I put my hand in his, he grips it tight. The kids and I are suddenly tired, hot, drained—and we look it, too.

It is warm out but with a soft, cool breeze that smells of trees, green juicy grass, flowers, and warm dirt.

We come to where the shoulder widens, and it opens up to about a hundred yards wide and that same distance in depth back away from the road. This area is flat and entirely covered with dusty, fine red dirt. As we had walked along this narrow road, the trees in the fields were sparse, but this dirt cut out from the road is thickly bordered by several types of trees.

Tucked all the way back is a small rectangular wooden building. It has a porch attached to the front with three wide steps going up to the porch.

Dad leads away from the road and toward this run-down-looking building, and the moment we step into that red, hot, dusty cutout, a horrible smell fills the air. The stench is a mix between nasty, hot, putrid garbage, and death. With each step the smells get worse. I notice that nowhere in this powdery dirt are there any other footprints or even tire marks. No one else has been here or wants to be here. I don't want to be here, and I begin to tell my dad that I don't want to go to that building. I become afraid, frantic almost. I want desperately to get back to that road, for us all to just keep walking anywhere but here.

Travis, Jacob, and Grace are now beside me. I can see they are afraid and questioning within themselves why their Papa was leading us here. The kids, with their hands over their noses like a filter for the stench, willingly continue forward. Not me. I pull and tug against Dad, trying to free myself from his grip, but he doesn't let go as I plead and beg him to take us back to the road. Calmly, all Dad says in response to my fretful pleas is, "Little Girl, you're alright," or, "That's enough now." All Dad ever had called me was Little Girl or Girlie when he was alive.

Third Dream

Up the few steps we go, and Dad grabs hold of the door handle with the kids all up next to him trustingly. The stench, that horrible, disgusting stench, is suffocating, but Dad doesn't seem to pay it any mind or to how I am leaned back, stretched out, pulling against his grip.

Dad opens the door and holds it open, telling Travis, Jacob, and HannahGrace to go in, giving them each a wink and a smile. They all, looking up at him, willingly step through. I now panic, tell my dad, "No!" But he doesn't care and responds with, "I told you to go in," and yanks me forward onto the door's threshold. Dad is not one to yell or get worked up, and he isn't now, but he is serious and gives me a look that says I'm fixin' to get my butt whipped.

As I am looking up at my dad, he lets go of my hand and nudges me forward with himself immediately behind me and closes the door so I can't turn around and leave.

Instantly, the air is cool, soft, clean, and has a lovely scent of roses and honeysuckle. The air is pure, and I can breathe! I look up and my children are all bright and refreshed looking and all smiles. There is a faint sound of some sort of melody in the distance. The building seems much bigger inside than it looks on the outside. The lighting is bright and clear, but not harsh. It has a peaceful feel to it.

Dad is standing in front of the door facing me. He tells me to look around, but I tell him I don't want to, that I just want to stand there by him. I ask him if we all can please just go back to the road and keep walking. He tells me that he wants me to look around here and that he will walk a bit with me.

Now I know he is going to leave me, and I see in my dad's eyes that he knows what I am thinking. I want out of here and for all of us to go back out into that rotting stench and endless travels, no matter how hard it may be. At least we would all be together.

My dad reaches out and strokes my hair. Then he puts my arm in his and leads me forward out into the room and away from the door.

The building has only this one open-spaced room, but furniture is placed throughout as divisions between areas. This place is filled with beautiful fabrics. There are all different sizes, colors, textures, and types of fabrics draped or folded and stacked over or on plush armchairs, or rich wood cabinets, such as China cabinets and armoires.

Dad points to different fabrics as we walk, asking me what I think of them. He sometimes stops for a moment to feel a piece of fabric that is draped over something, nudging me toward it. I stand silent, refusing to touch the fabric he holds out. So, he lets it go and leads me forward, walking slowly.

A beautiful young lady comes out from behind one of the dividers with a smile on her face. I know this woman. She was a worship leader at a church I had gone to. She does not know who the kids and I are, but she knows my dad and walks right up to him and tells him that she has been expecting him. My dad gives her a nod and a smile, simply saying, "Good." He then tells this beautiful woman, who smells of the fragrant roses and honeysuckle that fill the room—and that soft lovely melody I had been hearing seems to be coming out of her—that he wants me to have a dress, "a proper dress," he says. This lady tells my dad that she understands and reaches for my hand, saying, "I want to show you some fabrics."

Quickly I tighten my grip on Dad's arm and tell him that I don't want a dress and ask if we could please just go. The sweet young lady gives Dad a sympathizing look while still patiently holding her hand out to me, which I don't like.

Dad puts his hand over mine that is tight around his other arm and says, looking down at me, "I want you to have a dress. You'll need it." And then, looking at the young lady, he says, "Let's see what you had in mind."

The kids are relaxed but always near Dad and I, sticking close to one another. Dad talks with them, reaches out and pats their heads or gives a gentle stroke to one of their cheeks as we walk along. Dad also tells the beautiful lady that he wants "these two young fellas and the little one to have something special also made for them." He says this while giving a big smile and wink to Travis, Jacob, and HannahGrace.

Each time our fabric guide stops to show me or the kids samples she thinks we would like, my dad undoes my grasped grip around his arm and steps back. Again, I tell him that I don't want anything except for us all to leave together.

"Just look around," he responds.

Our guide tries to distract me with fabrics she holds up to me, but she is only getting on my nerves. Dad walks with me, smiles at me, and pets my hair, like he has always done, but then he inches away from me. I close up the gap between us fast and hold on to his shirttail.

"How come you are trying to leave me?" I frightfully ask.

"You're okay here, you all are, it's alright," he soothingly but authoritatively tells me.

Like I say, this whole place is filled with all sorts of fabrics and beautiful things, but soon Travis, Jacob, and HannahGrace each find a fabric bolt that is unmistakably set out just for them in the midst of all the others. Each of their individual fabrics is who they are. Somehow their chosen pieces show their hearts, their true strengths, courage, heartbreak, fears, but also their wisdom and faithfulness and joy.

Travis's and Jacob's chosen pieces are miraculously turned into unique shirt, vest, and jacket sets specifically tailored and detailed just for each of them. Grace's chosen fabric is turned into a simple but beautifully designed and fitted calf-length dress. These amazing children of mine are washed clean and transformed like Cinderella into the beautiful, confident people God created them to be without the evils and heartache of the world in our lives weighing them down.

Dad goes to each one of them, turns them around one by one, hugging and kissing them, and they him. He says to them, "There now, that's better, you reckon? I knew you'd find what was yours." He tells them that he loves them and, smiling, he hugs each one again.

Turning to me he says, "Now, Little Girl, it's your turn." I go right up to him, put my arms around him, hugging him tight, and tell him I don't need a dress. I just want him to stay with me. My dad puts his arms around me, hugging me tight, and kisses the top of my head. I relax, and then I feel him let out a long deep breath. He then lets me go with a wink and turns me around to face an area we have not walked through before. "I think something might be over here," he says and takes a few steps in that direction.

The beautiful fabric lady, who still does not acknowledge she knows us in real life, grabs my hand and leads me to a cabinet full of folded fabrics. I run back to my dad who is standing in the open area near the door. Crying, I tell him that I don't want him to go! "I know," he says quietly and takes me by the hand as I am still crying. He leads me back to where his helper was standing when she started to show me the fabrics before I ran to Dad.

The kids all come over to me in their glorious transformations. I tell them between sniffles how beautiful they each are and touch their cheeks. They go to the other side of their Papa because he is still holding my hand. Dad, the kids, and the lady all calmly touch or point out different fabrics to me. The more they all do this, the tighter I hold on to my dad. They must have all realized this, how afraid I am.

I am so broken feeling, lonely, and sad, not just from all that happened with losing Dad, but also from a difficult split from such an abusive husband and how terrible I and the kids, too, have been treated, lied about, and punished throughout this by so many people. People don't really know how heartbroken I am, and all the ways I have been and am still struggling.

My dad and the angelic fabric lady begin to casually talk to each other as though they really know each other, and somehow I think they do. The kids begin to be silly with each other. I am beginning now to look at the different fabrics around me and can see how pretty they all really are. I start to feel not so pressured or desperate, and with that I loosen my hand up within Dad's. He lets go of my hand. I look up at him and he winks at me and gives a slight nod. Dad doesn't walk away. He still stands next to me.

Looking over to my right on a hip-high, small, round pedestal table I see a stack of neatly folded fabric of all colors. There on top, with a silky, thin piece of cloth draped partly over it, is my fabric—the one for me. I step closer to the table, push the silky cloth away, and touch the fabric that is for me. I turn to Dad and say, smiling to

Third Dream

him, that I like this one. "I thought you would," he replies, as though he knew which one was for me all along. He pats my back and smiles.

The lady comes over to me and lifts the fabric up, unfolding it. The kids come beside me as I feel the fabric—it is soft, it is pretty, and I want it. The beautiful woman tells me I made a good choice. I turn back to my dad, holding on to a corner of my fabric for him to feel it, but my dad is gone. Looking back at the kids, my dream ends.

School photo of Junior as a teenager.

Junior in uniform after joining the U.S. Army at age 17, with his younger brother and his beloved mother.

Wedding of Junior Clay Taylor (18) and Kathy Elaine Blankenship (17) on December 14, 1973.

One of many awards Junior received throughout his driving career. This trophy was earned while in the Transportation Division of the Army, which he was in for six years.

Family photo while stationed in Germany.

Jenny (right) and her brother (left) dressed up with their dad (center).

Junior playing with all the grandkids at his home in Tullahoma, TN.

Junior walking with HannahGrace (7) during her brothers' birthday adventure in 2008.

JUNIOR CLAY TAYLOR

Work-related photo taken not long before Junior was killed.

Travis (16), Jacob (14), and HannahGrace (10) at their Papa's gravesite.

In the Rocky Mountains driving back from one of the trips to Tennessee to take care of business. Left to right: Travis, Jacob, Kathy (Mama/Nana, in the back), Miss Grace, and Jenny.

News Articles

THE FOLLOWING THREE ARTICLES are about my dad's murder case. Two are from the time when the crime was committed, and the third is the reportage from the plea deal in the courthouse. In these articles I am referred to as "Jenny Finney," but I have since gone back to my maiden name, Taylor. The articles are reproduced with permission from the *Tullahoma News* and the *Crossville Chronicle*.

"Man Found Stabbed in Burned House"
by Wayne Thomas.
Published Feb. 16, 2011

Taylor

Continued from Page 1A

ville, Ala.

THP officer Jack Alderman said Stewart apparently drove the car into a bridge on U.S. 127 South. He then allegedly got out of the car and tied a belt around his neck and to the bridge.

According to the report, he then jumped off the bridge, but the belt broke, dropping Stewart 30 to 40 feet into a small stream below.

Stewart was transported to Cumberland County Hospital and was later transferred to the University of Tennessee Medical Center in Knoxville, where he is undergoing treatment for critical injuries, according to the report.

Meanwhile, investigators from the fire marshal's office were sifting through the rubble Monday morning, attempting to determine what started the fire.

"The preliminary report from the state medical examiner shows that Taylor died of multiple stab wounds," Chief Blackwell said Tuesday.

Mr. Taylor was a U.S. Army veteran and owner-operator of JC Trucking.

His funeral services will be conducted at 1 p.m. Thursday at Moore-Cortner Funeral Home in Winchester.

(The Crossville Chronicle contributed to this story.)

Man Found Stabbed in Burned House
by Wayne Thomas – Staff Writer
published Feb. 16, 2011

Preliminary autopsy results indicate that a man whose body was found inside a partially burned mobile home at 1816 E. Lincoln St. Sunday died of multiple stab wounds, and an alleged suspect is in critical condition in a Knoxville hospital.

Tullahoma police have identified the victim as Junior Clay Taylor, 55. The suspect is identified as Stephen Floyd Stewart, 39, of Church Hill, Tenn.

Authorities believe the two are related.

According to reports, the Tullahoma Fire Department was dispatched to the home about 4:15 p.m. Sunday. After quickly extinguishing the blaze, firefighters entered the house and discovered Taylor's body.

They then summoned Tullahoma police, who began an investigation.

"We contacted the state fire marshal's office, and agents from Murfreesboro and Columbia arrived and assisted our investigators," Tullahoma Police Chief Paul Blackwell said Monday.

During the investigation, police were notified by the Tennessee Highway Patrol of a traffic accident in

Cumberland County where the driver had identification belonging to Taylor.

According to Cumberland County authorities, Stewart, of Church Hill, Tenn., was driving a Nissan Altima that had been reported as stolen in Huntsville, Ala.

THP officer Jack Alderman said Stewart apparently drove the car into a bridge on U.S. 127 South. He then allegedly got out of the car and tied a belt around his neck and to the bridge.

According to the report, he then jumped off the bridge, but the belt broke, dropping Stewart 30 to 40 feet into a small stream below.

Stewart was transported to Cumberland County Hospital and was later transferred to the University of Tennessee Medical Center in Knoxville, where he is undergoing treatment for critical injuries, according to the report.

Meanwhile, investigators from the fire marshal's office were sifting through the rubble Monday morning, attempting to determine what started the fire.

"The Preliminary report from the state medical examiner shows that Taylor died of multiple stab wounds," Chief Blackwell said Tuesday.

Mr. Taylor was a U.S. Army veteran and owner-operator of JC Trucking.

His funeral services will be conducted at 1 p.m. Thursday at Moore-Cortner Funeral Home in Winchester.

(*The Crossville Chronicle* contributed to this story.)

The body of Junior Clay Taylor, 55, was found inside this partially-burned home Sunday afternoon by Tullahoma firefighters.

Preliminary autopsy results indicate he died of multiple stab wounds. At right, working the scene, from left, are Lt. Jason Damron, and volunteers Raymie Hill and Rodney Duncan.

Photo by Sam Crimm II

'The preliminary report from the state medical examiner shows that Taylor died of multiple stab wounds.'

—Tullahoma Police Chief Paul Blackwell

NEWS ARTICLES

"Crash Turns into Suicide Attempt"
by Michael R. Moser.
Published Feb. 15, 2011

Crash Turns into Suicide Attempt
by Michael R. Moser
published Feb. 15, 2011

[Photo text: The driver of this car attempted to hang himself from the Byrd's Creek bridge after the car left the road. Local police say victim might be tied to a homicide in Coffee County.]

What was first reported as a car leaving a bridge and crashing into the creek below, seconds later turned into a report of a man attempting to hang himself from the bridge, and now investigators believe the chain of events might be linked to a brutal homicide in Coffee County.

Trooper Jack Alderman identified the motorist turned suspect as Stephen Floyd Stewart, 37, of Church Hill in Hawkins County.

The Tennessee Highway Patrol and Cumberland County emergency response crews were dispatched at 7:24 p.m. to the bridge spanning Byrd's Creek on Hwy. 127 S, just south of the Tennessee Department of Transportation garage, on a report of a vehicle running off the side of the bridge and into the creek.

Moments later, with emergency crews and law enforcement racing to the scene, a second call came into the emergency communications center reporting that the motorist had run to the top of the bridge and was attempting to hang himself.

A passing motorist told the Chronicle that as she drove by the scene, she observed a woman in night clothes standing on the bridge, distraught and crying, saw a police officer looking over the side of the bridge and then saw people running down to the water.

The woman, who was not identified by authorities, lives nearby and heard the crash. She went outside to investigate, called authorities and then witnessed his suicide attempt.

Deputy David Bowman was one of the first to arrive on the scene and waded into the creek to keep the victim's head above water. Emergency crews assisted in removing him from the cold water.

Alderman reported that when he arrived, the woman who reported the crash quoted Stewart as stating, "I am not going back to prison." He made reference to something he had been involved in earlier in the day.

Stewart was rushed by ambulance to Cumberland Medical Center and later transferred to The University of Tennessee Medical Center for injuries suffered in the fall.

The vehicle Stewart was driving, a late model Nissan Ultima, had been reported stolen in Huntsville, AL, on Saturday. The owner told police that she had left her vehicle running to warm up and that when she looked back outside, it was gone.

THP investigated the crash and then turned over the scene to Cumberland authorities who stood by until the Coffee County and Tullahoma investigators arrived.

After authorities identified Stewart, they learned that he was wanted for questioning in connection with a homicide in Tullahoma.

Sunday afternoon the Tullahoma Fire Department was dispatched to Lincoln St. in that city on a report of a mobile home on fire. The fire was extinguished and the body of the resident, identified as Junior Taylor, 45, was discovered, according to the Tullahoma News and Guardian.

Taylor had been stabbed multiple times and may have had his throat slashed. His body has been sent to Nashville for an autopsy.

The Tullahoma newspaper is also reporting that Stewart was convicted in connection with the stabbing and robbery of a Deckerd, TN, man in 2005.

Cumberland County Sheriff's Department remained on the scene to as did Assistant District Attorney Amanda Hunter to assist Tullahoma and Coffee County investigators.

NEWS ARTICLES

"Stewart Pleads Guilty to Murder of Uncle"
by Wayne Thomas
Published Sept. 13, 2013

Notes from Jenny: This article mislabeled Junior Taylor as "uncle"—he and Stewart were second cousins. Also, I am misquoted as saying "No one deserves to die"—we all die at some point. I remember saying, "No one deserves to die like that." Finally, this article states the murder took place February 11th, but it was on February 13th.

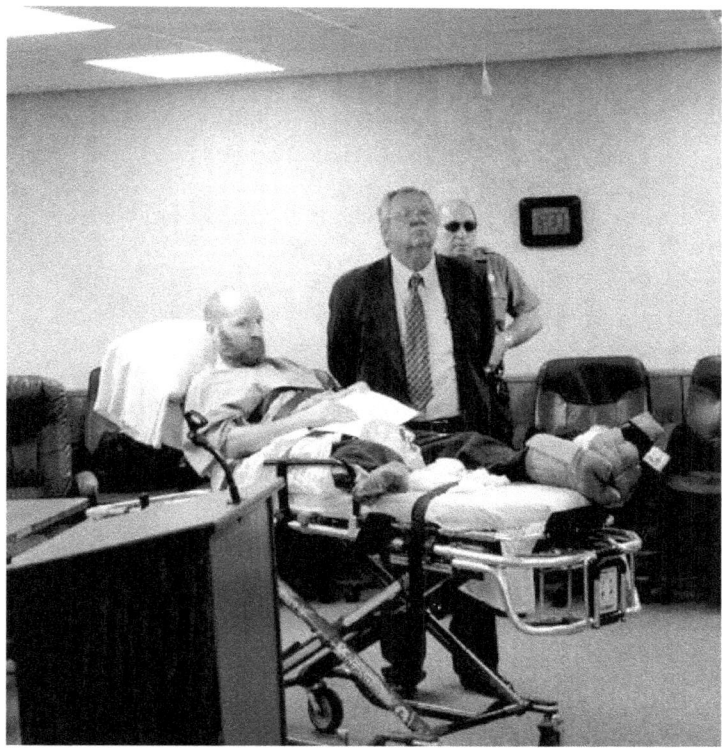

Stephen Stewart, on gurney, appears in Coffee County Circuit Court Tuesday afternoon to plead guilty to the murder of Junior Clay Taylor, of Tullahoma, in February 2011. Stewart, who is paralyzed and had a leg amputated, was rolled into the courtroom to enter his plea. His attorney Kevin Askren stands next to the gurney and sheriff's Capt. Donnie Thomas looks on.
—Staff Photo by Wayne Thomas

A Church Hill man was sentenced Tuesday to a maximum of 35 years in the Tennessee Department of Corrections for the February 2011 murder of a Tullahoma man.

Stephen Floyd Stewart, 40, pleaded guilty in a Coffee County courtroom to the Feb. 11, 2011 murder of his uncle, Junior Clay Taylor, and of then setting the man's East Lincoln Street mobile home on fire.

He pleaded guilty to second-degree murder, theft of over $1,000, attempted arson and aggravated robbery charges.

According to Coffee County Assistant District Attorney Kristy West, Stewart and Taylor "got into an argument" and, after some time, Stewart grabbed a kitchen knife and stabbed the victim 40 times.

"He then removed a wallet from the victim and took $4,066 in cash from it," the prosecutor told Circuit Court Judge Vanessa Jackson.

According to West, Stewart then went to an outside shed, got a container of gasoline and poured gas throughout the residence, setting it on fire.

After setting the house on fire, Stewart then allegedly left the area in a Nissan Altima that he had taken from a resident of Huntsville, Ala. He drove to Cumberland County, where police say that he ran the car off a bridge on Highway 127.

According to testimony presented Tuesday, Stewart then left the car and ran to the top of the bridge and tried to hang himself with a belt. However, the belt broke and he plunged into the creek below.

When Stewart fell into the creek he landed on a rock and broke his back and is now paralyzed. Since his arrest, Stewart had a leg amputated and suffers from numerous other health problems, according to information presented at court on Tuesday.

Stewart was transported to the Coffee County Justice Center via ambulance from the Deberry Special Needs facility in Nashville. He entered the courtroom on a gurney and faced Judge Jackson to enter his pleas.

After entering his pleas, Stewart then tearfully addressed Taylor's daughter, Jenny Finney, who was in the courtroom, telling her he "was sorry for what he had done."

He told her that he didn't know what happened to him, saying that he had "just snapped."

"Please forgive me. I'm sorry," he said.

Finney then addressed Stewart, telling him that he was not "created to be a murderer." She stated that she had to forgive him, but no one deserves to die.

"God loves you and you have to ask him to forgive you," Finney said. "You have hurt a lot of people," Finney said.

Stewart was represented by attorneys Margo Kilgore and Kevin Askren.

After the court proceeding, he was returned to the Deberry Special Needs facility where he will continue serving his sentence.

"In You, O Lord, I put my trust; let me never be ashamed; deliver me in Your righteousness. Bow down Your ear to me, deliver me speedily; be my rock of refuge, a fortress of defense to save me. For You are my rock and my fortress; therefore, for Your name's sake, lead me and guide me. Pull me out of the net which they have secretly laid for me, for You are my strength. Into Your hand I commit my spirit; you have redeemed me, O Lord God of truth."

Psalm 31:1–5

www.ingramcontent.com/pod-product-compliance
Lightning Source LLC
Chambersburg PA
CBHW071214160426
43196CB00012B/2300